CAPE®
ART AND DESIGN UNIT 1

FOUNDATIONS OF ART AND DESIGN

MULTIPLE-CHOICE QUESTIONS & ANSWERS *with* EXPLANATIONS

FOSTER'S

THE LEADER IN EXAM PREPARATION

CAPE® QUESTIONS & ANSWERS SERIES

FOSTER'S CAPE® Questions & Answers Series gives students the tools to practise and refine their exam techniques over time. It is an ideal revision aid to assist students through their CAPE® Exams. The books under this series come in both Multiple-Choice Questions and Answers and Essay Questions and Answers. They provide full coverage of the CAPE® syllabuses clearly and logically.

Check out Q&As books in the following subjects: -

Accounting
Art and Design
Biology
Caribbean Studies
Literatures in English
Economics
Entrepreneurship
Food and Nutrition
Geography
Green Engineering
History
Law
Literatures in English
Management of Business
Physical Education & Sport
Physics
Pure Mathematics
Sociology
Tourism

FOSTER'S

THE LEADER IN EXAM PREPARATION

CAPE®
ART AND DESIGN UNIT 1

FOUNDATIONS OF ART AND DESIGN

MULTIPLE-CHOICE
QUESTIONS & ANSWERS
with EXPLANATIONS

REMONE L. FOSTER

RLF Publications.
"... redefining publishing..."
Kingston * Jamaica

CAPE®

ART AND DESIGN UNIT 1

FOUNDATIONS OF ART AND DESIGN

MULTIPLE-CHOICE QUESTIONS & ANSWERS
A Study Material for CAPE® Students

Published in Jamaica by
RLF Publications Limited
2nd Floor, 52 Duke Street, Kingston CSO, Jamaica, W.I.
www.rlfpublications.com
books@rlfpublications.com

ISBN: **978-976-97179-8-5**

Cover and book design by RLF Publications Limited
Typeset by RLF Publications Limited

CONTENTS

A. PREFACE

Multiple-choice questions are designed to assess a wide range of content and knowledge and form an integral part of the overall assessment of the CAPE® Art and Design Examination. Numerous students are not fond of these questions, however, once they are prepared, they are likely to do well. The essential aim of this book is to prepare students for the multiple-choice questions component of their exam. When used properly, this book will allow them to understand the instructions and format of the exam, and to get keen critical thinking skills over time. In preparing this book, a lot of consideration was given to the needs of the students, the content of the CAPE® Art and Design syllabus and the types of multiple-choice questions asked on the exam.

Practice ensures that students are well-prepared when it comes to multiple-choice questions. It is through consistent practice that they will do well. This book offers them practice in reading and following instructions, practice in pacing themselves, and most importantly, practice in answering the types of multiple-choice questions that will be asked on the exam.

B. KEY FEATURES OF THIS BOOK

Key features of this book include: -

- a Diagnostic Test that mirrors the actual CAPE® Art and Design - Paper 01;
- a Mock Examination at the end of the book;
- 9 Practice Exams overall;
- over 300 multiple-choice questions that cover the entire CAPE® Art and Design syllabus;
- multiple-choice questions in all topic areas;
- an answer key for the Diagnostic Test, Mock Examination and each Practice Exam;
- explanations for answers for the Diagnostic Test, Mock Examination and each Practice Exam;
- a student-friendly and easy-to-use approach to preparing for exams;
- complete coverage of the CAPE® Art and Design syllabus;
- a detailed bibliography for further reading; and
- a 3-week Exam Plan

C. HOW TO BEST USE THIS BOOK

As with all study guides, this book should not replace your textbooks or be used in isolation of them. It is highly recommended that you consult your textbooks for additional information and use your syllabus as a checklist while using this book. Most students are inclined to cram at the last minute and this is quite risky when preparing for a multiple-choice questions exam. You will find that there is a lot of content to cover, and if left at the last minute, you are likely to become confused, frustrated and discouraged. Therefore, it is recommended that you start to use this book early and continue using it throughout the year. Time management is also crucial, and you should try and set aside some uninterrupted time to practise using the strategies in answering the questions in this book and assess yourself.

At the beginning of the book, you will find a Diagnostic Test which you are to complete before proceeding any further in the book. You can attempt this test as many times as you want until you are comfortable with your assessment. Thereafter, you will find five Practice Exams. Invite your teachers to use this book within the classroom and seek their opinions on items that you are uncertain about. The best approach is to attempt the questions, review your answers by reading the explanations given at the end of the Practice Exams and then consult your textbooks on the topics that you are not comfortable with.

At the end of the book, you will find a Mock Examination which will give you one final assessment. When it comes time to take your exam, you will be in the best position to ace the multiple-choice questions.

D. TO THE STUDENTS

Most students are nervous when it comes to multiple-choice questions. This is reasonable since such questions offer no room to manipulate a response and the correct answer is predetermined and surrounded by convincing distractors. Multiple-choice questions are not always straightforward and at the advanced level, students are required to interpret data and apply essential critical thinking skills. Preparing for a multiple-choice questions exam is more than recalling terms, concepts or definitions. It involves understanding these terms, concepts and definitions and applying them to different proses and narratives. However, with consistent practice, you will be able to master the strategies of answering these questions.

The questions asked on the multiple-choice questions paper are carefully written in accordance with the CAPE® Art and Design syllabus. By this, the questions are intended to assess the range of content covered by the syllabus and it is therefore important that a total coverage of the syllabus is done. Of course, there is a benefit to this. Although you may be asked a question you simply do not know the answer to, it is unlikely that the examiner would ask you a question on a topic that is not on the syllabus.

You are advised to complete the Diagnostic Test at the beginning of the book before proceeding to the other sections of the book. The Mock Examination at the end of the book is to be taken under exam conditions and will be your final assessment before the real exam.

E. TO THE TEACHERS

The role of any teacher is to prepare their students for their examinations. However, it is a difficult task to prepare students for multiple-choice questions exams. For this reason, most teachers may ignore the responsibility altogether and insist that their students read the textbooks. However, preparing for a multiple-choice questions exam is more than memorizing theories, principles, generalizations, dates, names, events and concepts. It involves strategies that must be mastered over time.

Teachers ought to feel confident that in encouraging their students to use this book, their students will be able to understand and master the various strategies used when answering multiple-choice questions. This book ensures that strategies are learnt and employed. Teachers are encouraged to take time and go through the multiple-choice questions in this book with their students and in doing so, strengthen their confidence in answering and interpreting questions.

F. ASSESSMENT

Paper 01 of the CAPE® Art and Design Examination consists of 40 compulsory multiple-choice questions that cover Module 1 on the syllabus. The paper has a total of 40 marks, contributes **20%** of the overall grade and lasts for **1½** hours (90 minutes).

You will be assessed based on your knowledge and understanding of the content of Module 1 of the CAPE® Art and Design syllabus. Perhaps, more importantly, is your ability to apply this knowledge to the relevant questions. The questions asked are aimed at testing the recall of basic information, terms, concepts and generalizations; analysing and interpreting arts; and testing your understanding of various art forms, techniques, artistic expressions and cultural issues.

G. ANATOMY OF A MULTIPLE-CHOICE QUESTION

While you may have done several multiple-choice questions exams over the years, you may still be oblivious to the construct of these questions. It is important to understand the construct of these questions as this will improve the way you approach them. Essentially, a multiple-choice question consists of two parts: the problem (***stem***) and a list of suggested answers (***alternatives***).

The stem can manifest itself in several forms, perhaps as a question, an extract or an incomplete sentence. The stem tells you what you should look for in the answer. The alternatives will consist of one correct response (***i.e. the answer to the stem)*** and a number of other wrong responses (***i.e. the distractors***). The distractors can be very convincing and aim to distract you from picking the correct response. Consider the example below:

	Which artistic technique involves creating designs by cutting and glueing paper onto a surface?	**STEM**
Distractor	(A) Collage	**ALTERNATIVES**
Answer	(B) Decoupage	
Distractor	(C) Origami	
Distractor	(D) Papier-mâché	

The correct answer is B. Decoupage is an artistic technique that involves cutting out designs or images from paper and glueing them onto a surface, often combined with additional layers of varnish or lacquer to create a decorative effect. Although the other options involve paper, they can be distinguished. Collage (A) is an artistic technique that involves assembling various materials, such as paper, fabric, photographs and found objects, onto a surface to create a composition. These

materials are often cut or torn and then arranged and glued onto a support, such as canvas or paper, to form a new image or design. Origami (C) is the art of paper folding. It involves creating intricate and often three-dimensional objects by folding a single sheet of paper without cutting or glueing. Origami is known for its precision and can be used to create various shapes, animals, and objects through a series of folding techniques. Papier-mâché (D) is a technique that involves creating objects or sculptures by layering paper strips or pulp soaked in a paste or adhesive, such as a mixture of water and glue. The paper is shaped and moulded over a framework or armature, and once it dries, it becomes hard and can be painted or decorated. Papier-mâché is often used to make masks, piñatas, and other crafts.

H. QUESTIONS ON THE CAPE MULTIPLE-CHOICE QUESTIONS EXAM

The examiners use a variety of questions. You may find questions that ask you to look for the best response or ask you to find the exception or least likely response. Questions may be based on an illustration, cartoon or some other form of visual. It may also be based on a quotation, an extract or even an incomplete statement. Generally, there are three (3) types of questions that are asked on your multiple-choice questions exam: **recall questions, analytical (or evaluative) questions and interpretative questions.**

Recall questions

You will find that a majority of the questions on the paper are just recall questions. By this, you are asked to recall basic information, concepts, names or principles. They are generally straightforward and non-analytical. By this, you are not required to look beyond the information that you have learnt about the subject matter mentioned in the stem. These questions may be in the form of an incomplete sentence or a statement. An example may be:

Which of the following techniques is commonly used in Optical Art?

(A) Pointillism
(B) Collage
(C) Airbrushing
(D) Trompe-l'oeil

The correct answer is A. Optical Art, also known as Op Art, is an artistic movement that emerged in the 1960s. It focuses on creating optical illusions and visual effects through the use of geometric patterns, shapes, and colours. One of the key techniques used in Optical Art is pointillism. Pointillism is a technique in which small, distinct dots or points of colour are applied to a surface to create an image. The viewer's eyes blend the dots together, creating the illusion of continuous colours and forms. This technique allows the artist to play with perception and create visual effects that give the impression of movement, depth, and vibration. While collage (B), airbrushing (C), and trompe-l'oeil (D) are artistic techniques used in various art forms, they are not commonly associated with Optical Art. Collage involves assembling different materials or images to create a composition, airbrushing involves using an airbrush

tool to apply paint, and trompe-l'oeil is a technique used to create realistic illusions that deceive the viewer's perception.

Analytical (or evaluative) questions

An analytical (or evaluative) question requires that you analyse or evaluate data. Often, you are asked to make inferences from your knowledge of a certain subject. With such questions, you may be required to critically think about the factors that have led to an event or systematically conceptualize a specific idea, period or investigation. An ideal example of this type of question may be:

Which of the following materials were commonly used by the Taino people in their artistic creations?

I. Stone and clay
II. Wood and bark
III. Ceramic and textiles
IV. Feathers and shells

(A) I and III only
(B) I, II and IV only
(C) II, III and IV only
(D) I, II, III and IV

The correct answer is D. Items I, II, III and IV are materials that were commonly used by the Taino people in their artistic creations. Stone, clay and ceramic were commonly used for creating pottery, sculptures, and other ceramic objects. Wood and bark were utilized for carving intricate designs on items such as masks, utensils, and canoes. Feathers and shells were incorporated into adornments, jewellery, and ceremonial attire.

A question can be both recall and analytical. By this, the question requires the recall of basic facts, however, these facts will not assist you unless you can make specific inferences about a particular concept or subject. In approaching these questions, it is also important to consider the keywords used in the questions. These words can guide you in analysing and evaluating the material. An ideal example of this type of question may be:

What criticism was generally levelled against European artists who painted art in the Caribbean during the pre-emancipation period?

(A) They were often indifferent to the plights of enslaved people
(B) They were mainly interested in the landscape and natural beauty of the Caribbean
(C) They were primarily interested in capturing the families of white planters
(D) They did not give adequate insight into colonial life

The correct answer is A. The criticism levelled against European artists who painted Caribbean society during the pre-emancipation period is that they often displayed indifference to the suffering of enslaved people. Many European artists focused on depicting picturesque landscapes, exotic flora, and fauna of the Caribbean, while frequently disregarding or minimizing the harsh realities of slavery and the suffering endured by the enslaved population. Their portrayals tended to romanticize Caribbean life, emphasizing idyllic scenes and the privileged lifestyles of plantation owners and the white elites. This approach not only ignored the injustices faced by enslaved people but also perpetuated a distorted view of Caribbean society. Critics argue that these European artists failed to address or acknowledge the hardships and oppression experienced by the enslaved individuals, who were an integral part of Caribbean society during that period.

Interpretative questions

A question may ask that you interpret data. Such a question may be in the form of an extract, a quotation, an illustration, a map, a chart or even a table. You are required to apply your knowledge to the available data. An ideal example of an interpretative question is based on the extract below.

The item below refers to the image below which depicts a wooden artefact called a "duho" created by the Taino people in the pre-Columbian period.

Image is in the public domain.
Source: https://commons.wikimedia.org/wiki/File:Duho.jpg
(retrieved 30th November 2024)

Which of the following factors does not adequately explain why the artefact in the diagram can be classified as art?

(A) Aesthetic value and creativity
(B) Utilitarian function
(C) Historical significance and age
(D) Cultural and social context

The correct answer is B. The factor that does not adequately explain why the artefact in the image can be classified as art is utilitarian function. The artefact depicted is a wooden object called a duho created by the Taino people in the pre-Columbian period. The duho was primarily used as a ceremonial item, specifically a seat or throne for the caciques (chiefs) of the Taino society. While the artefact does have a utilitarian function as a ceremonial seat or throne, the classification of an object as art goes beyond its practical function and takes into account factors such as those at options (A), (C) and (D). The duho can be considered art because it exhibits aesthetic qualities, such as intricate carvings and design elements, which are often associated with artistic expression and creativity. Additionally, the classification of the duho as art can be supported by its historical significance and age. It is a pre-Columbian artefact representing a specific cultural and historical context. Lastly, understanding the cultural and social context of the duho is important in recognizing its artistic value. It reflects the artistic traditions and practices of the Taino people, and it carries cultural and symbolic meaning within their society.

I. HOW TO STUDY FOR MULTIPLE-CHOICE QUESTIONS EXAMS

It is important to develop a study method that corresponds to the way you work. Perhaps you cannot work under pressure, you are a slow reader, you cannot memorize simple facts, or you cannot cram at the last minute. In preparing for a multiple-choice questions exam, you may need to study ahead of time and manage your time carefully. Since you are required to have extensive coverage of the entire syllabus, you should try not to cram. It begins by participating in class, taking notes and creating a study schedule. Perhaps it is best to study by topics at weekly intervals. In preparing for your exam, keep in mind that:

(i) **Practice is important**. Accordingly, try and find practice exams, past tests (if available) or study guides that can help you practise answering multiple-choice questions. This book offers ideal practice questions.

(ii) **Review your class notes meticulously**. It is important to take good notes before and during your lectures. Thereafter, you go through these notes and confirm their accuracy by reverting to your textbooks. Sometimes, you may want to rewrite your notes or type them in a more legible manner. The aim is to organize your notes so that they can be easily memorized.

(iii) **Learn the material**. You may find that it is easier to memorize theories, facts, names or concepts when you understand the material that you are studying. When you wait until the last minute, your mind is only concerned with memorizing the information and not learning it. On your exam, you are not required to recite information, you are simply asked to recognize the correct answer and ignore the distractors.

(iv) **Get a study partner**. Some students find it much easier to work alone, however, having a study partner can be ideal. You can quiz each other and develop your own questions and flashcards. Furthermore, you can try and explain different concepts and facts to your partner which will improve your ability to memorize these concepts and facts.

(v) **Review your marked scripts**. Some students are not fond of doing a post-mortem on their exam scripts. However, if your scripts are available to you, you should examine your incorrect answers to know how to move forward. Perhaps you made simple mistakes which can be improved over time. Insist that your teachers review the answers with you.

J. STRATEGIES FOR ANSWERING MULTIPLE-CHOICE QUESTIONS

A tabulating machine will assess your answers for the multiple-choice questions paper. The machine merely records the correct answers – it does not care how you arrived at that answer; it does not care that you guessed the answer; it does not care how long it took you to arrive at the answer; and it certainly does not care that you knew the answer after just one read of the question. The rationale behind this is that while you are required to have sufficient knowledge of the content of your syllabus to do well, it really boils down to the strategies used to arrive at your answers. There are numerous strategies that you can master, and which will allow you to display your knowledge. Since you cannot bluff your way through a multiple-choice questions exam, it is important to understand and utilize these strategies.

Reading

Time is of the essence; however, this does not mean that you should race through the exam paper. It is always important to read the directions and questions carefully. In reading the questions too quickly, you may skip important words or phrases that are crucial in guiding you to the correct answer. Accordingly, when reading the questions, you may want to consider: the type of words used, the time frame of the question, whether any words are italicized, capitalized or bolded, the language used, the tense or even the subject-verb agreement. Important words or phrases can be underlined or circled so that you can find exactly what you are looking for.

For difficult questions, a good strategy is to paraphrase the stem in a way that you can understand it. You may even find it useful to cover the options, read the question and try to answer the question before looking at the options. By doing this, you may be less inclined to fall prey to the convincing distractors among the options. It is also important to keep your mind open as you read the questions. As you proceed, the questions or options given for a question may trigger your memory about another question.

Identifying keywords

Although it was mentioned under "reading", identifying keywords in a question is an important strategy by itself. You should pay special attention to ***negatives*** ("none", "not", "neither", "except", "least"); ***superlatives*** ("most", "most likely", "best", "all", "only"); ***relative qualifiers*** ("usually", "often", "generally", "may"); and ***absolute qualifiers*** ("always", "never", "every'). Keep in mind the following:

- When a negative word is used, if the answer choice option is true then it is not the correct answer. The negative usually requires that you select the answer choice that is wrong;

- Answer choice options that use absolute qualifiers are less likely to be correct than those that use relative qualifiers. This is because relative qualifiers allow for exceptions and are usually correct, while absolute qualifiers do not allow for exceptions and are usually wrong.
- Questions that ask you to choose the "BEST" answer require that you not only look for a correct answer but the best of the options. It follows then that the best answer is one that must be true all of the time, in all cases and without exceptions. Sometimes, the best answer is the one that encompasses the other options or explains the options. It is usually the one that is the most inclusive.
- Questions that begin with the superlative, "All" ends with the negative "Except". By this, the correct response would be the option that is wrong or is least likely to be true.

Pacing

You are required to answer 45 multiple-choice questions within 2 hours. It means therefore that you can at least spend a little over two minutes on each question. This may seem like a small amount of time, but by pacing yourself properly, you should be able to answer all of the questions within the specified time and may even have enough time to review your work. One of the main aims of this book is to ensure that you develop a pacing scheme that corresponds with the way you work. Therefore, it is important to take the Diagnostic Test.

In pacing yourself, you should read all of the questions, answer those that are easy for you and leave those that are difficult to return to. The key rule is that you should never spend all of your time on difficult questions. When you meet such questions, read them and jot down any clues that you have that may assist you in answering them. Thereafter, put an "**X**", an asterisk (*) or a check (✓) beside the questions and move on to other questions. You can then return to those questions later. Of course, if you are shading in your answers on the answer sheet simultaneously, you should remember to skip the answer ovals for those questions skipped.

Elimination

Elimination is one of the most important strategies for answering multiple-choice questions. So important is this strategy that you use it without even knowing. Your mind is systematically programmed to skip those answer choices that are wrong. Elimination is the most effective way of improving your chances of selecting the correct answer to a question. Simply put, if you can successfully eliminate two of the answer choices, then you have increased your chances of getting the correct answer from 25% to 50%.

You are required to read the questions carefully. Thereafter, try and pinpoint those answer choices that you know are illogical, funny or simply incorrect. The incorrect answer is one that misrepresents a fact, ignores the central issue in the question or uses faulty reasoning. Naturally, you may be required to consider the subtle differences between the answer choices.

Educated Guessing

There are certainly going to be some questions that you will not know the answers to even if you are very familiar with the topic. Since you are not penalized for getting a question wrong, it makes perfect sense to guess the answer. Educated guessing is an important strategy that utilizes the other strategies mentioned thus far. In truth, you are not really guessing the answer and perhaps a better description would be "*intelligent deduction.*" It involves systematically rejecting those answer options that you know are definitely wrong and then guessing the answer based on those answer options that remain. Of course, you must read the questions carefully and discard choices that are wrong, illogical or simply unrelated to the subject. Thereafter, make a conscious decision as to which of the remaining choices appears most correct. In this regard, trusting yourself is very important. As a key rule, let your first choice remain unless you are absolutely sure that you were wrong.

Other simple strategies

(a) Responses that are funny, absurd or illogical are generally wrong.

(b) "All of the above" is usually the correct response, once you can verify that more than one of the other responses is probably correct.

(c) "None of the above" is generally the wrong answer.

(d) The longest response is generally the correct answer because the examiners tend to load it with qualifying adjectives or phrases in an attempt to clarify it. By this, it contains elaborations necessary to make it correct.

(e) If you are guessing a very difficult question, the correct response is most likely (b) or (c). The examiners subconsciously think that the correct answer is "hidden" better if it is surrounded by distractors. Response (a) is usually the least likely to be the correct answer.

(f) If two (2) options are opposite to each other, chances are one of them is the correct answer. This is called the "echo-option." Similarly, if two choices seem similar then neither of them is likely to be the answer.

(g) The stem and the answer choice selected must agree grammatically.

(h) All parts of an answer choice must be correct for the answer to be correct.

(i) It is important not to panic. When you panic you are devoid of reason and tend to rely on your instinct rather than knowledge. While trusting your instinct is important, you must still understand the exam content. When you panic, your memory is inhibited and your ability to think is compromised. You may start to overlook keywords and facts and become confused. It is best to stay calm.

(j) When shading your answer ovals, shade the oval completely but stay within the oval, shade the answer oval for one question at a time, don't make a slash (/) or an **X**, and use a #2 or a 3B pencil. These pencils are ideal because the lead is not too dark and not too light, and they are not too hard or too soft.

K. THE DIAGNOSTIC TEST

At the beginning of this book, you will find a Diagnostic Test that can be likened to a mock examination. This test mimics the instructions and layout of the multiple-choice questions paper for the CAPE® Art and Design Examination. It consists of 40 questions, based on Module 1. This test is a vital part of the book, and it is highly recommended that much attention is paid to it before proceeding to the other sections.

Why take the Diagnostic Test?

Taking the Diagnostic Test is of paramount importance and ties in neatly with the purpose of this book, which is to allow you to become more familiar with the examination. In taking the Diagnostic Test, you will be able to:

- understand and appreciate the format of the exam;
- get familiar with the instructions of the exam;
- pace yourself so that you can answer all of the questions on the exam;
- identify, understand and appreciate your strengths and weaknesses when taking multiple-choice questions exams; and
- appreciate the areas of your studies that need to be improved.

How to take the Diagnostic Test?

The Diagnostic Test mimics the actual exam; therefore, you must take the test as if you were taking the real exam. For that reason, you are expected to take the Diagnostic Test under exam conditions and should set aside 90 minutes of uninterrupted time. When the time is up, all work **MUST STOP**. This is important because if you were not able to complete all 40 questions within the allocated 90 minutes, then there is a need to better pace yourself. After you have completed the test, you should use the answer key provided at the end of the Diagnostic Test to assess your work.

Do not be too concerned if you do not do as well as you want to, as the aim of the Diagnostic Test is merely to get you in the mood. Besides, if you already know everything, then you probably do not need this book. During your assessment, you must consult the **"Explanations for Answers"**, which is located at the end of the test. Even if your answers are correct, it is still best to look at the explanations, as you will probably receive additional information that can aid you in effectively answering such questions, no matter what form they may present themselves in on the real exam paper. At the end of taking the Diagnostic Test, you will come to terms with your weaknesses and strengths. You may find that there is a need to pay more attention to a particular topic, or perhaps there is a need to pace yourself better.

L. THE MOCK EXAMINATION

At the end of this book, you will find a Mock Examination. This is an exam taken before a final exam or an official exam to assess a student's readiness. You will note that just like the Diagnostic Test at the beginning of the book, it mimics the instructions and layout of the multiple-choice questions paper for the CAPE® Art and Design Exam. This test is a vital part of the book as it assesses your level of preparation for the actual exam.

It is highly recommended that it is taken under exam conditions. You should set aside 90 minutes of uninterrupted time because if you are not able to complete all 40 questions within the allotted 90 minutes, then additional work needs to be done to get you ready.

The Mock Examination is extremely useful for students looking to do well on their official CAPE® Art and Design Exam. It is important to leave the Mock Examination until you have completed all the other aspects of the book.

Why take the Mock Examination?

The Mock Examination is tied neatly into the overall purpose of this book, which is to get you ready for the actual multiple-choice questions component of the exam. In taking the Mock Examination:

(a) you will get a feel of the real exam and it provides a trial run to determine your progress;
(b) you will get rid of any pre-exam jitters because it will put you in the same feeling and situation as the actual exam;
(c) you will revise the entire syllabus in the context of an examination;
(d) you will get good practice, and this will enhance your ability to perform well on the exam; and
(e) you will become familiar with exam conditions.

At the end of the day, it is hoped that in completing this book and the Mock Examination, your confidence in taking the official CAPE® Art and Design Exam will be enhanced. The Mock Examination should make you feel more confident and as your confidence builds, you will believe in yourself and your ability to do well.

M. THE 3-WEEK EXAM PLAN

This book is a quick revision aid. While it is recommended that you start using this book from early in the school year, it is designed in such a way that it can get you exam-ready within 3 weeks. Here is a quick 3-week Exam Plan to get you exam ready.

WEEK 1	**Monday**	Attempt Diagnostic Test under exam conditions • *Review the answers and explanations for answers*
	Tuesday	Attempt Practice Test 01 • *Review the answers and explanations for answers* • *Review textbooks for more information*

	Wed.	Review Diagnostic Test and Practice Test 01
	Thursday	Attempt Practice Test 02 • *Review the answers and explanations for answers* • *Review textbooks for more information*
	Friday	Review Diagnostic Test and Practice Test 02
	Saturday	Review textbooks
WEEK 2	**Monday**	Attempt Practice Tests 03 and 04 • *Review the answers and explanations for answers* • *Review textbooks for more information*
	Tuesday	Review Practice Tests 01, 02 and 03
	Wed.	Attempt Practice Tests 05 and 06 • *Review the answers and explanations for answers* • *Review textbooks for more information*
	Thursday	Continue review of textbooks
	Friday	Review Diagnostic Test and Practice Test 06
	Saturday	Attempt Practice Test 07 • *Review the answers and explanations for answers* • *Review textbooks for more information*
	Sunday	Continue review of textbooks
WEEK 3	**Monday**	Practice Tests 04 and 05 • *Review the answers and explanations for answers* • *Review textbooks for more information*
	Tuesday	Review Practice Tests 01 and 02
	Wed.	Continue review of textbooks
	Thursday	Attempt Mock Examination under exam conditions • *Review the answers and explanations for answers*
	Friday	Review Diagnostic Test and Mock Examination
	Saturday	Review Practice Tests 01, 02 and 03
	Sunday	Review Practice Tests 06 and 07

Check out Q&As books in the following subjects: -

Accounting
Art and Design
Biology
Caribbean Studies
Literatures in English
Economics
Entrepreneurship
Food and Nutrition
Geography
Green Engineering
History
Law
Literatures in English
Management of Business
Physical Education & Sport
Physics
Pure Mathematics
Sociology
Tourism

CAPE®

ART AND DESIGN UNIT 1

DIAGNOSTIC TEST

Paper 01
1 hour 30 minutes

READ THE FOLLOWING INSTRUCTIONS CAREFULLY.

1. This Diagnostic Test consists of 40 items.

2. You will have 1 hour and 30 minutes to answer them.

3. Each item in this Diagnostic Test has four suggested answers lettered (A), (B), (C) and (D). Read each item and decide on the best choice. Look at the sample item below.

Sample Item:

Which weaving technique involves tying and dyeing sections of the yarn to create a pattern before weaving?

(A) Batik
(B) Ikat
(C) Embroidery
(D) Macramé

Sample Answer:

The best answer to this item is "Ikat" and so (B) is shaded.

4. When you are told to begin, turn the page and work as quickly and as carefully as you can. If you cannot answer an item, go on to the next one and return to this item later.

RLF Publications.
"... redefining publishing..."

1. Which of the following artists is likely to use the technique of chiaroscuro?

(A) Ceramicist
(B) Painter
(C) Photographer
(D) Sculptor

2. Which of the following artists is known for the use of the sfumato technique during the Renaissance period?

(A) Pablo Picasso
(B) Vincent van Gogh
(C) Leonardo da Vinci
(D) Salvador Dalí

3. Sir Anthony Musgrave was instrumental in establishing the premiere institutions for the promotion and preservation of Jamaican art and culture. This institution is

(A) The Institute of Jamaica
(B) The National History Museum of Jamaica
(C) The National Gallery of Jamaica
(D) The African Caribbean Institute of Jamaica

4. Everyday ornaments found in Indigenous households in the Caribbean were often made of

(A) Copper and bronze
(B) wood and stones
(C) limestones and marbles
(D) gold and guanine

5. Which of the following was NOT associated with Mayan architecture?

(A) Stepped platforms
(B) Stone buildings
(C) Floating gardens
(D) Masonry structures

6. Which of the following was traditionally used for creating lithographic prints?

(A) Wood and oil-based ink
(B) Stone and oil-based ink
(C) Clay and oil-based ink
(D) Canvas and oil-based ink

7. Which of the following Caribbean islands is known for its vibrant tradition of storytelling, featuring characters such as Anansi the spider?

(A) Barbados
(B) Jamaica
(C) Guyana
(D) Montserrat

8. Which art movement was heavily influenced by African art and culture, and rejected traditional European art forms?

(A) Impressionism
(B) Expressionism
(C) Fauvism
(D) Cubism

9. What is the purpose of the ribbed vault in Gothic architecture?

(A) To provide structural support
(B) To add decorative elements to the ceiling
(C) To let in natural light
(D) To provide ventilation

10. What is one advantage of being a self-taught artist?

(A) They have a greater understanding of art history and theory
(B) They are more likely to be successful in the art world
(C) They have the freedom to develop their own unique style
(D) They have more opportunities for formal exhibitions and shows

Items 11 and 12 refer to the image below.

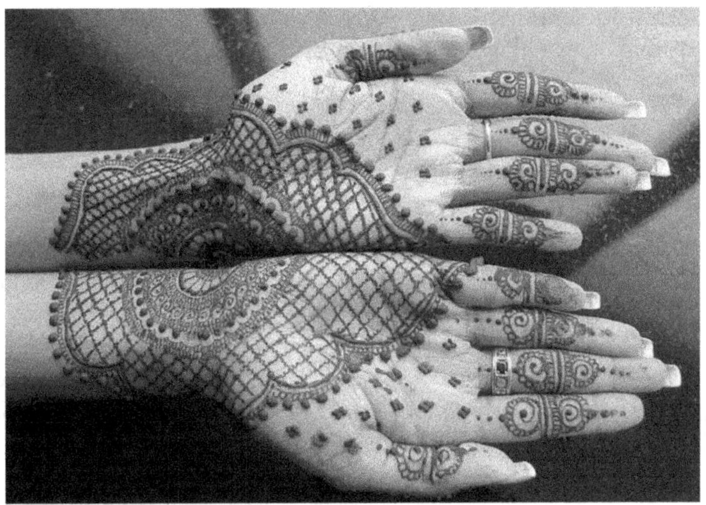

Image is in the public domain. Retrieved from www.wikipedia.com (30th November 2024)

11. The art practice that is displayed in the image refers to

(A) mehndi
(B) pattachitra
(C) camouflage
(D) tattoos

12. Which of the following Caribbean countries is usually associated with the art practice illustrated in the image?

(A) Barbados and St. Lucia
(B) Guyana and Trinidad and Tobago
(C) Jamaica and Grenada
(D) Grenada and Montserrat

13. What is the BEST way in which sports inspire art?

    (A) By representing physical beauty and athleticism
    (B) By creating a sense of community and national identity
    (C) By embodying the principles of teamwork and competition
    (D) By exploring cultural and social issues related to sports

14. Which religion heavily influenced the iconography and symbolism in Haitian art?

    (A) Rastafari
    (B) Santeria
    (C) Vodou
    (D) Comfa

15. Which of the following BEST describes performance art?

    (A) A form of art that involves creating static visual artworks
    (B) A genre of art that focuses on the use of dramatic literature
    (C) An artistic practice that combines various art forms such as theatre, dance, and visual arts
    (D) An art form that combines visual and kinetic art

16. Which of the following BEST accounts for the recognition of Morn Trois Pitons in Dominica as a World Heritage Site by UNESCO?

    (A) The presence of diverse racial groups
    (B) The presence of diverse natural features
    (C) The presence of diverse cultural artefacts
    (D) The presence of diverse military architecture

17. The Caribbean artist Canute Caliste who was known for vibrant intuitive painting hailed from

    (A) Kingston, Jamaica
    (B) Nassau, Bahamas
    (C) Havana, Cuba
    (D) Carriacou, Grenada

18. All of the following textile weaving techniques were likely employed by Indigenous people in the Caribbean EXCEPT

    (A) Needlepoint weaving
    (B) Loop weaving
    (C) Finger weaving
    (D) Backstrap weaving

19. Which of the following materials was commonly used in basketry by Indigenous Caribbean societies?

    (A) Synthetic fabric
    (B) Plant fibres
    (C) Tobacco leaves
    (D) Flaxen threads

20. The critical theory of art posits that

    (A) art is created through a variety of techniques
    (B) art should be visually stimulating and aesthetically pleasing
    (C) art is based on technical skill and craftsmanship
    (D) art is to be understood through social, cultural and political lens

21. Which of the following techniques involves creating a pattern by carving away parts of a clay surface that has been covered with a layer of slip?

(A) Mishima
(B) Slip trailing
(C) Wax resist
(D) Sgraffito

22. Which Caribbean country is known for its carnival celebrations that incorporate traditional folklore characters such as the Jab Jab and the Dame Lorraine?

(A) Jamaica
(B) Trinidad and Tobago
(C) Barbados
(D) Haiti

23. What was the purpose of Georgian architecture in the Caribbean?

(A) To showcase the wealth and power of colonial rulers
(B) To provide comfortable living quarters for the enslaved population
(C) To blend European and African architectural styles
(D) To incorporate local materials and building techniques

Items 24 and 25 refer to the image below which relates to a form of art that was likely created by the indigenous people of Puerto Rico in the pre-Columbian era.

Image © 2003 Todos los Derechos Reservados and used pursuant to the Creative Commons Licence via www.en.wikipedia.org. Source: http://www.icp.gobierno.pr/aye/simposio.htm

24. The art form depicted in the diagram is

(A) petroglyph
(B) calligraphy
(C) pictography
(D) hieroglyphics

25. Based on the image, what inference can be drawn about the subject matter of indigenous art in the Caribbean?

(A) Spirals and geometric patterns
(B) Human figures and portraits
(C) Abstract shapes and forms
(D) Natural figures and symbols

---

26. Realism emerged as a reaction against which art movement?

(A) Romanticism
(B) Baroque
(C) Abstract Expressionism
(D) Pop Art

27. Which is true of the Caribbean Art Movement?

(A) It originated outside of the Caribbean
(B) It involved artists solely within the Caribbean
(C) It excluded artists from the Caribbean diaspora
(D) It had little impact outside of the Caribbean

28. Which of the following BEST describes a stencil?

(A) A technique used to create textured surfaces on a canvas
(B) A method of creating 3D sculptures using layers of paper or cardboard
(C) A design cut out of a material, such as paper or plastic, to be used as a template
(D) A process of applying multiple layers of paint to create a gradient effect

29. The Caribbean's Museum of Rum (Musée du Rhum) which is known for a collection of old distilling equipment is located in

(A) Haiti
(B) Cuba
(C) Martinique
(D) Montserrat

30. What might tourists expect to see at the Musée du Panthéon National Haïtien (Museum of the National Pantheon of Haiti) (MUPANAH)?

(A) A series of elaborate sculptures by Indigenous people who resided in Haiti
(B) A garden museum that displays different plants and shrugs native to Haiti
(C) A mausoleum (tomb) for important figures in Haiti's history
(D) An array of exhibits, artwork and artefacts related to all aspects of Haitian history

31. Which is NOT a likely purpose of basketry in indigenous Caribbean societies?

(A) Storing food
(B) Crafting weapons
(C) Transporting materials
(D) Decorating spaces

32. Which of the following European artists is known for painting plantation life in Suriname?

(A) Paul Gauguin
(B) Henri Matisse
(C) Dirk Valkenburg
(D) Rembrandt van Rijn

33. The artist who is generally considered the "mother of modern Jamaican art" is

(A) Edna Manley
(B) Ebony Patterson
(C) Hope Brooks
(D) Gloria Escoffery

34. What is the term for an artist who is trained in a specific artistic tradition or style?

(A) Classical
(B) Contemporary
(C) Avant-garde
(D) Experimental

35. Which Hindu festival is celebrated in Trinidad and Tobago with colourful powder and water throwing?

(A) Holi
(B) Diwali
(C) Navratri
(D) Durga Puja

36. What is the significance of the serpent in Haitian Vodou iconography?

(A) It represents evil and danger
(B) It represents fertility and regeneration
(C) It represents healing and medicine
(D) It represents wisdom and knowledge

37. What is the name of the plant commonly used to make baskets in the Caribbean?

(A) Bamboo
(B) Mangrove
(C) Palm
(D) Papyrus

38. Which of the following natural dyes produces a bright red colour?

(A) Indigo
(B) Cochineal
(C) Annatto
(D) Henna

39. What are colonial artefacts in the Caribbean?

(A) Items made by Indigenous people during colonial rule
(B) Items made by European colonizers during colonial rule
(C) Items made after the colonial era
(D) Items from ancient Caribbean civilizations

Item 40 refers to the image below which represents a sculpture by Edna Manley entitled Beadseller.

Source: https://nationalgalleryofjamaica.wordpress.com/2014/09/08/in-retrospect-section-2-seminal-exhibitions/edna-manley-beadseller/ (retrieved 30th November 2024)

40. Which of the following is the MAIN art style utilized?

(A) Kinetic art
(B) Modernism
(C) Cubism
(D) Impressionism

END OF TEST

ANSWER KEY FOR THE DIAGNOSTIC TEST

Item No.	Answer Key
1.	B
2.	C
3.	A
4.	B
5.	C
6.	B
7.	B
8.	D
9.	A
10.	C
11.	A
12.	B
13.	D
14.	C
15.	C
16.	B
17.	D
18.	A
19.	B
20.	D

Item No.	Answer Key
21.	D
22.	B
23.	A
24.	A
25.	D
26.	A
27.	A
28.	C
29.	C
30.	D
31.	B
32.	C
33.	A
34.	A
35.	A
36.	B
37.	C
38.	B
39.	B
40.	B

EXPLANATIONS FOR ANSWERS FOR DIAGNOSTIC TEST

1. **(B)** Chiaroscuro is a technique that involves contrasting light and shade in drawing and painting. As such, it is likely that a painter would use this technique. It is generally used to create a sense of depth, volume and drama by strategically placing areas of light and shadow to enhance forms, shapes, contours and spaces. Painters generally use this technique to give paintings a three-dimensional quality with some areas brightly illuminated while other areas plunged into deep shadows. They can use brushes, palette knives, or other tools to apply and manipulate paint, which allows them to create the desired chiaroscuro effects. While it is not unlikely that other artists such as ceramists (A), photographers (C) and sculptors (D) might use light and shadow in their work, the technique of chiaroscuro is particularly associated with painting and drawing.

2. **(C)** Leonardo da Vinci is famously known for the use of the sfumato technique during the Renaissance period. Sfumato is an Italian word that means "smoky" or "blurred." As such, this is a painting technique in which subtle transitions between colours and tones are used to create soft, hazy, and almost imperceptible edges. One of da Vinci's most notable paintings using this technique is the Mona Lisa, which is known for its soft blending of colours, delicate modulation of light and shadow, and overall ethereal quality of the subject's face. The other painters, while renowned in their respective periods, are not specifically known for the sfumato technique. Picasso (A) is associated with cubism and surrealism. Van Gogh (B) is known for his expressive brushwork and bold colours; Dali (D) is associated with surrealism.

3. **(A)** Sir Anthony Musgrave is known for the establishment of the Institute of Jamaica (IOJ) in 1879. The IOJ plays a vital role in the promotion and preservation of Jamaican art and culture. However, it also focuses on literature, science and education. It now encompasses various divisions and departments dedicated to different areas of study and promotion in Jamaica such as the National Gallery of Jamaica, the National History Museum of Jamaica, the National Museum of Jamaica and the African Caribbean Institute of Jamaica. The National Gallery of Jamaica, in particular, is the country's leading art gallery and museum. While options (B), (C) and (D) are considered divisions of the IOJ, they were not established by Sir Anthony Musgrave.

4. **(B)** Ornaments found in Indigenous households in the Caribbean were often made of materials that were readily available in their environment and suited to their crafting skills. Indigenous Caribbean peoples such as the Taino and Kalinago frequently used wood and stones for making ornaments due to their abundance and ease of working with these materials. The other options are not likely to be used for everyday ornaments. Copper and bronze (A) and limestones and marbles (C) were not commonly used by indigenous Caribbean peoples. While gold and guanine (a gold alloy) were used, especially for ceremonial items, they were not as commonly found in everyday household ornaments.

5. **(C)** The Mayans were skilled architects and builders, and their distinctive architecture encompassed a wide range of structures, such as ceremonial temples, stepped platforms, pyramids, palaces, ball courts and residential buildings. Options (A), (B) and (D) were aspects of Mayan architecture. Stepped platforms and stone buildings were used for temples and pyramids which often used masonry techniques such as mortar, stucco, and intricate stone carvings. Floating gardens (or chinampas) (C) were associated with Aztec society. These gardens were unique to Tenochtitlan which was surrounded by water. Aztec farmers and architects constructed large gardens that seemingly floated above the water.

6. **(B)** Lithographic prints were traditionally created using stone and oil-based ink. Lithography is a printing technique that was invented in the late 18th Century and was referred to as "stone writing." It relied on the principle that oil and water do not mix. In the original lithographic process, a smooth limestone or a specifically prepared lithographic stone was used as the printing surface. The image was drawn or transferred onto the stone using greasy materials such as crayons, tusche, or ink. The greasy marks repelled water when the stone was dampened. After the image was prepared on the stone, an oil-based ink was applied to the surface. The oil-based ink adhered to the greasy image while it repelled water from the non-image areas. A sheet of paper was then pressed onto the inked stone, and the image was transferred onto the paper. The stone acted as a matrix for creating multiple prints because it could have been reinked and reused to produce multiple copies of the image. This process typically allowed for precise and detailed reproduction of the original image.

7. **(B)** Jamaica has a rich cultural heritage that includes a strong tradition of storytelling. One of the most famous characters in Jamaican folklore is Anansi, the spider who is known for his cleverness and wit. He is often depicted as a cunning and mischievous figure who uses his intelligence to outsmart other characters. Anansi stories have been passed down through generations in Jamaica and have become an integral part of the island's oral tradition. These stories involve Anansi getting into various humorous, and often moral, dilemmas with valuable life lessons woven into the narratives.

8. **(D)** Cubism is an art movement that emerged in the early 20th Century in which artists sought to depict objects from multiple viewpoints by fracturing and reassembling them in geometric forms and facets. It was heavily influenced by African art and culture, particularly the aesthetic qualities of African masks and sculptures. In many ways, it rejected traditional European art forms and transformed the way artists represented and perceived reality. Artists such as Pablo Picasso and Georges Braque were inspired by the geometric forms, simplified shapes, and expressive power found in African masks and sculptures. Impressionism (A), Expressionism (B) and Fauvism (D) were not inspired by African art and culture.

9. **(A)** Ribbed vaults were essential in Gothic architecture for providing structural support. They allowed for the distribution of weight and the construction of higher and more complex ceiling structures, enabling the development of the iconic tall, thin walls and large windows of Gothic cathedrals. Options (B), (C) and (D) do not align with the purpose of ribbed vaults in Gothic architecture. While ribbed vaults can contribute to the aesthetic appeal of Gothic interiors, their primary purpose is

structural. Additionally, ribbed vaults themselves did not directly let in natural light. However, their use enabled the inclusion of larger windows, which allowed more natural light to enter the building. Finally, ribbed vaults were not designed to provide ventilation.

10. **(C)** One advantage of being a self-taught artist is that they have the freedom to develop their own unique style. Self-taught artists often have the freedom to explore and develop their artistic skills and style without formal constraints or prescribed methods. They are not bound by traditional rules or techniques taught in formal art education, which allows them to experiment, innovate, and find their own artistic voice. By relying on their own intuition, observation, and self-guided learning, self-taught artists have the opportunity to develop a distinct artistic style that is authentic and unique to them. This ability to develop a personal artistic style can be seen as an advantage as it allows self-taught artists to stand out and create work that is distinct and original. It can contribute to their artistic identity and make their work more recognizable and memorable. While self-taught artists may not have formal training in art history and theory (A), and their path in the art world may present challenges (B), they can still achieve success and recognition through their unique style and artistic vision. Furthermore, formal exhibitions and shows (D), may also be available to self-taught artists depending on their opportunities and recognition within the art community.

11. **(A)** The art form displayed in the image refers to mehndi, also known as henna. It is a traditional form of body art that originated in ancient cultures and is widely practised in many countries, particularly in South Asia, the Middle East, and North Africa. Mehndi involves the application of a paste made from the leaves of the henna plant to create decorative designs on the skin. The art of Mehndi has a long history and cultural significance. It is commonly associated with celebrations and special occasions, such as weddings, festivals, and religious ceremonies. Mehndi is often applied to the hands and feet, but it can also be applied to other parts of the body. In the Caribbean, mehndi holds cultural and symbolic significance for people of East Indian descent. It is often considered a symbol of beauty, auspiciousness, and celebration. The process of applying mehndi is also seen as a form of artistry and creativity, with skilled mehndi artists showcasing their talent through intricate and elaborate designs.

12. **(B)** The art of mehndi is deeply rooted in South Asian culture, and its popularity has extended to various parts of the world where South Asian communities have settled. In the post-emancipation period, a large number of East Indians came to the Caribbean as indentured servants, most of whom settled in Guyana, Trinidad and Tobago and Suriname. As such, Mehndi is largely associated with these Caribbean territories due to the presence of a large East Indian population in these countries.

13. **(D)** Sports can have a significant influence on art by inspiring visual representations such as paintings, sculptures, and photographs that capture the energy, movement, and emotions associated with athletic events, as well as influencing literature, fashion, and even architecture through the culture and aesthetics of various sports. One of the best ways in which sports inspire art is by exploring cultural and social issues related to sports. Indeed, sports intersect with various cultural, social, and political aspects of

society. Artists may use sports as a platform to address broader themes and shed light on societal issues such as race, gender, identity, and social justice. While options (A), (B) and (C) are also ways in which sports can inspire art, option (D) is more comprehensive and can encompass elements of the other options. Notwithstanding, it is the individual artist's interpretation and their ability to effectively communicate their inspiration through their artwork that determines the impact and significance of sports-inspired art.

14. **(C)** The religion that heavily influenced the iconography and symbolism in Haitian art is Vodou. Vodou is a syncretic religion that originated in Haiti and is practised by a significant portion of the Haitian population. It blends elements of West African religions brought to the Caribbean during the transatlantic slave trade with Catholicism and other influences. In Haitian art, particularly in the context of religious and spiritual artwork, Vodou symbolism and iconography are prevalent. Vodou deities, spirits, and mythological figures are depicted in paintings, sculptures, and other forms of artistic expression. These artworks often feature vibrant colours, intricate patterns, and symbolic representations associated with Vodou beliefs and practices. Options (A), (B) and (D) are also syncretic religions in the Caribbean but are not associated with Haiti. Rastafari is associated with Jamaica; Santeria is associated with Cuba; and Comfa is associated with Guyana.

15. **(C)** Performance art is a genre of art that encompasses a wide range of artistic practices, often involving live performances by the artist or performers. It is characterized by the incorporation of elements from various art forms, such as theatre, dance, music, visual arts, and even everyday actions or interactions (C). The other options do not completely describe performance art. Unlike traditional static visual artworks (A), performance art is ephemeral and typically occurs in the presence of an audience. It often involves the artist or performers actively engaging with the viewers, creating a unique and immersive experience. Furthermore, while performance art may include elements of dramatic literature (B) in some instances, it is not limited to the use of scripted texts. Performance art can involve improvisation, physical movement, gestures, sounds, spoken words, and other forms of expression to convey artistic ideas and concepts. Finally, performance art goes beyond the combination of visual and kinetic elements (D) to encompass a broader range of art forms and creative practices.

16. **(B)** The recognition of Morn Trois Pitons in Dominica as a World Heritage Site by UNESCO is due to the presence of diverse natural features. Morn Trois Pitons is a mountainous area located in Dominica in the Caribbean. It was designated as a World Heritage Site by UNESCO in 1997 due to its outstanding natural significance. The site is known for its diverse and unique natural features, which include volcanic peaks, geothermal features, freshwater lakes, and dense rainforests. UNESCO recognizes and protects sites of exceptional cultural or natural value. In the case of Morn Trois Pitons, its recognition as a World Heritage Site is primarily based on the presence of diverse natural features that are considered significant on a global scale. The site represents a remarkable example of volcanic and geothermal activity, showcasing the island's geological history and biodiversity. The recognition as a World Heritage Site also helps to raise awareness of its ecological importance and promotes sustainable management and conservation efforts. While Dominica, like many Caribbean countries, has diverse racial groups (A) and cultural artefacts (C) and might have some military architecture (D), these factors are not the primary reasons for the recognition of Morn Trois Pitons as a World Heritage Site.

17. **(D)** The Caribbean artist Canute Caliste (1914-2005) hailed from Carriacou, Grenada. Caliste was known for his expressive and colourful artwork, often characterized as intuitive painting. His art reflected the vibrant spirit and cultural heritage of the Caribbean region. Caliste's work can now be found in numerous large collections worldwide.

18. **(A)** The textile weaving technique that was NOT likely employed by Indigenous people in the Caribbean is Needlepoint weaving. Needlepoint weaving, also known as needle weaving or needlework, involves using a needle and thread to create designs and patterns on a fabric or canvas. This is a more modern technique and it is unlikely that indigenous Caribbean people had access to this method or the necessary materials for this method to be feasible. On the other hand, loop weaving (B), finger weaving (C), and backstrap weaving (D) are all techniques that have been historically used by indigenous peoples in the Caribbean and have played an essential role in the region's textile traditions and cultural heritage. Loop weaving involves creating fabric by pulling loops of yarn or thread through other loops. Finger weaving is a method where the fabric is woven using only the fingers, without the need for a loom. Backstrap weaving is a technique where a weaver uses a simple loom consisting of a strap around the weaver's waist and another attached to a fixed object, creating tension to weave intricate patterns.

19. **(B)** Indigenous Caribbean societies traditionally made baskets using plant fibres. These fibres were often derived from plants such as palm trees, sisal, seagrass, and other natural plant materials. The specific types of plants and fibres used varied among different indigenous groups and depended on the availability of local resources. Plant fibres were chosen for their strength, flexibility, and suitability for weaving. Skilled artisans would gather, process, and prepare the fibres to create intricate and functional baskets. The techniques of weaving and basketry were passed down through generations, and baskets served various purposes, including storage, carrying goods, and as cultural artefacts. In contrast, synthetic fabric (A) and flaxen threads (D) were not commonly used in traditional indigenous Caribbean basketry. Synthetic fabrics are a modern invention and were not available to indigenous societies in the past. Flaxen threads, which typically refer to linen made from flax, were not commonly found in the Caribbean, and the indigenous peoples primarily relied on locally available plant fibres. Tobacco leaves (C) were used for various purposes by indigenous Caribbean societies, but they were not typically used in basketry. Tobacco leaves had cultural and ceremonial significance, often being used for smoking or in spiritual practices, rather than as a material for weaving baskets.

20. **(D)** Critical theory in art focuses on examining and understanding art within broader social, cultural, and political contexts. It seeks to analyse the power dynamics, ideologies, and social structures that shape artistic production, reception, and interpretation. According to critical theory, art is not solely judged based on the techniques used (A), its visual qualities (B) or technical skill (C). Instead, it is to be

seen as a product and reflection of the social and cultural conditions in which it is created. The theory further emphasizes the role of art in challenging existing power structures, questioning dominant narratives, and promoting social change. Accordingly, critical theorists often explore issues such as representation, identity, gender, race, class, and political ideologies in art. They aim to uncover hidden meanings, ideologies, and power dynamics embedded within artistic works and institutions. They also encourage viewers and scholars to engage critically with art, considering its social, cultural, and political implications.

21. (D) The technique that involves creating a pattern by carving away parts of a clay surface that has been covered with a layer of slip is sgraffito. Sgraffito is a decorative pottery technique where a layer of slip, which is a liquid clay mixture of water and clay, is applied onto a clay surface. Once the slip has partially dried but is still moist, the artist uses various tools like knives, needles, or other sharp objects to scratch or carve through the slip layer, revealing the contrasting clay body underneath. By selectively removing parts of the slip layer, the artist can create intricate patterns, designs, or textures on the clay surface. The contrast between the slip and the exposed clay creates visually appealing and textured effects in the finished piece. The other options can be distinguished. Mishima (A) is a technique that involves inlaying slip or another contrasting material into incised or impressed lines on the clay surface. Slip trailing (B) is a technique where slip is applied in a controlled manner using a nozzle or brush to create raised lines or designs on the clay. Wax resist (C) is a technique where wax is applied to specific areas of the clay surface to create a barrier and prevent glaze or slip from adhering to those areas during firing.

22. (B) The Caribbean country known for its carnival celebrations that incorporate traditional folklore characters such as the Jab Jab and the Dame Lorraine is Trinidad and Tobago. Trinidad and Tobago is renowned for its vibrant and colourful carnival festivities, which are among the most famous and widely celebrated in the Caribbean. The carnival in Trinidad and Tobago is deeply rooted in the country's cultural heritage and showcases a fusion of African, Indian, and European influences. During the carnival, various traditional folklore characters come to life, including the Jab Jab and the Dame Lorraine. The Jab Jab, also known as "Devil Mas," involves individuals covering themselves in black oil, molasses, or tar-like substances, and wearing horned helmets or devil-like costumes. The Jab Jab is often seen dancing to the beat of steelpan music and is considered a representation of resistance and liberation. The Dame Lorraine, also known as the Fancy Sailor, is a costumed figure adorned with colourful and extravagant attire, representing a blend of European and African cultural influences. The character often wears an oversized mask, oversized hoop skirts, and carries a parasol. The Dame Lorraine is known for its playful and satirical portrayal of social and political themes.

23. (A) Georgian architecture was prevalent during the Georgian era, which spanned from the early 18th Century to the mid-19th Century. This architectural style was heavily influenced by the neoclassical designs of ancient Greece and Rome. In the Caribbean, Georgian architecture was adopted and promoted by colonial rulers, such as the British and the French. Georgian buildings in the Caribbean often featured symmetrical facades, classical proportions, and decorative elements such as columns, pediments, and ornate detailing. They were designed to evoke a sense of grandeur and sophistication, reflecting the tastes and aspirations of the ruling class. By this, the purpose of constructing Georgian-style buildings in the Caribbean was to demonstrate the wealth, prestige, and power of the colonial elites. Options (B), (C) and (D) do not explain the initial purpose of Georgian architecture in the Caribbean.

24. **(A)** The art form depicted in the diagram is a petroglyph. These are rock carvings or engravings made by removing or incising the surface of a rock to create images or symbols. It is likely that the indigenous people of Puerto Rico (the Taino) created petroglyphs by carving or pecking directly into the surface of a rock using stone chisels. The other options do not describe the art form in the diagram. Calligraphy (B) refers to the art of decorative handwriting or lettering, often associated with specific writing systems such as Chinese, Arabic, or Japanese calligraphy. Pictography (C) refers to a system of communication or writing that uses pictorial symbols or images to represent words, ideas, or concepts. It is an ancient form of writing that predates the development of more complex writing systems like hieroglyphics. Hieroglyphics (D) specifically refers to a writing system, which uses a combination of pictorial symbols, phonetic signs, and ideograms.

25. **(D)** Based on the image, which depicts a bird, it can be inferred that the subject matter of Indigenous art in the Caribbean often includes representations of natural elements, such as animals, plants, landscapes, and natural phenomena. Indigenous people in the Caribbean had a deep connection to their natural surroundings and often incorporated these elements into their artistic expressions. They may have used symbols, motifs, or stylized depictions of nature to convey cultural beliefs and spiritual concepts or to celebrate the natural world that surrounds them. This can be seen in various forms of indigenous art, including pottery, basketry, sculpture, and textiles.

26. **(A)** Realism, as an artistic movement, emerged in the mid-19th Century as a response to the Romantic movement that preceded it. Romanticism emphasized imagination, emotion, and idealized representations of the world. It often depicted fantastical or sublime scenes, focusing on the individual's subjective experience. In contrast, Realism sought to represent the world as it is, without idealization or embellishment. Realist artists aimed to depict everyday life, ordinary people, and the social realities of the time. They focused on portraying the objective truth and accuracy in their artistic representations. Realism was influenced by various factors, including social and political changes, the rise of industrialization, and advancements in science and technology. Realist artists believed in portraying the social conditions and struggles of the working class, shedding light on the inequalities and injustices of their time.

27. **(A)** The Caribbean Art Movement, also known as the Caribbean Artists Movement (CAM), was initiated in England during the 1960s and 1970s. It was a collective effort by Caribbean artists who were residing in England at the time and focused on the works of Caribbean writers, visual artists, poets, dramatists, filmmakers, actors and musicians. The movement aimed to provide a platform for Caribbean artists in England to explore their cultural heritage, address issues of identity, and challenge the prevailing narratives and stereotypes associated with the Caribbean. It sought to promote a sense of unity, cultural pride, and recognition for Caribbean artists living in the diaspora. While the movement originated in England, it also had connections and resonances with the Caribbean itself. Many of the artists involved in the Caribbean Art Movement had Caribbean roots and drew inspiration from their cultural heritage and experiences in the region. The movement served as a means of bridging the Caribbean and its diaspora through artistic expression and dialogue. Options (B), (C) and (D) are not true of the Caribbean Art Movement.

28. (C) A stencil refers to a design or pattern that has been cut out of a material, such as paper, cardboard, or plastic. The stencil is used as a template through which paint, ink, or another medium can be applied to create a repeated image or pattern on a surface. To use a stencil, it is placed on the desired surface, and then paint or ink is applied over the stencil, either by brushing, spraying, or stippling. The cut-out areas of the stencil allow the paint or ink to pass through, transferring the design onto the surface. The result is a replicated image or pattern that can be repeated multiple times. Stencils are commonly used in various artistic and practical applications. They can be used for creating designs on walls, fabric, furniture, paper, and many other surfaces. Stencils provide a way to achieve precise and consistent shapes or patterns, making them a popular tool for artists, crafters, and even in industrial applications.

29. (C) The Caribbean's Museum of Rum (Musée du Rhum) is located in Martinique, which is known for its production of rum. The Musée du Rhum is a museum dedicated to showcasing the history, production, and cultural significance of rum in Martinique. The museum features a collection of old distilling equipment, artefacts, and exhibits that provide insight into the rum-making process, the different types of rum, and the historical importance of rum in Martinique and the wider Caribbean region. Visitors to the Musée du Rhum can learn about the island's rum-making traditions, explore the exhibits on display, and even participate in rum tastings. The museum offers a comprehensive experience that highlights the cultural and historical significance of rum in Martinique's heritage.

30. (D) Musée du Panthéon National Haïtien (Museum of the National Pantheon of Haiti) (MUPANAH) is a museum in Haiti dedicated to preserving and showcasing the history and culture of the country. The museum features a diverse collection of exhibits that cover different periods and themes of Haitian history. The exhibits at MUPANAH may include historical artefacts, artworks, photographs, documents, and interactive displays that provide insights into the rich and complex history of Haiti. The museum also features a collection of mausoleums or tombs that house the remains of prominent Haitian figures, including political leaders, military heroes, writers, and artists. Through these exhibits, tourists can gain a deeper understanding of Haiti's past, its struggles and achievements, its cultural heritage, and its contributions to the Caribbean and the wider world.

31. (B) Basketry played a vital role in indigenous Caribbean cultures for practical purposes such as gathering, storing, and transporting various items, particularly food. Indigenous peoples of the Caribbean used baskets made from natural materials like plant fibres, reeds, or vines to harvest and store fruits, vegetables, grains, and other food resources. Baskets were woven in various sizes and shapes, depending on their specific use. They also provided a means of carrying harvested crops from the fields, storing food in homes, and transporting goods within communities. The woven structure of baskets allowed for ventilation and kept the stored food fresh for longer periods. Beyond their functional use, baskets in indigenous Caribbean societies also held cultural significance. They were often decorated with intricate patterns, designs, and natural dyes, showcasing the artistic skills and cultural aesthetics of the makers. Additionally, basketry techniques and designs were passed down through generations, contributing to the preservation of traditional knowledge and craftsmanship.

32. **(C)** Dirk Valkenburg was a Dutch artist who visited Suriname in the 18th Century. During his time in Suriname, he depicted various aspects of plantation life, including scenes of enslaved people, plantation owners, and the landscape of the region. His paintings captured the social and cultural dynamics of Suriname during the colonial era. Valkenburg's works provide valuable insights into the historical context of Suriname, documenting the plantation system, the lives of enslaved individuals, and the interactions between different social groups in the colony. His paintings are considered significant visual records of the time and contribute to our understanding of the history and visual representation of Suriname.

33. **(A)** The artist who is generally considered the "mother of modern Jamaican art" is Edna Manley. She was a Jamaican sculptor and artist who played a pivotal role in the development of modern Jamaican art and was instrumental in promoting and advocating for the recognition of Jamaican art and culture. Manley's work often depicted themes related to Jamaican identity, social justice, and the struggles of marginalized communities. Her sculptures, paintings, and drawings captured the spirit and essence of Jamaican life, and she actively sought to incorporate local elements and African influences into her art. In addition to her artistic contributions, Edna Manley was also involved in cultural and educational initiatives. She co-founded the Jamaica School of Art (now known as the Edna Manley College of the Visual and Performing Arts) and was an influential figure in the formation of the National Gallery of Jamaica. Her significant contributions to the art scene in Jamaica and her efforts to establish a distinct Jamaican artistic identity have led to her being recognized as the "mother of modern Jamaican art."

34. **(A)** The term for an artist who is trained in a specific artistic tradition or style is classical. A classical artist refers to an artist who adheres to the established principles, techniques, and styles of a particular artistic tradition or historical period. They often receive formal training in traditional artistic disciplines, such as drawing, painting, sculpture, or other art forms, and aim to create work that aligns with the standards and aesthetics of that tradition. Classical artists may draw inspiration from the works of renowned artists of the past, study and replicate traditional techniques, and strive for technical excellence and mastery within the chosen style or tradition. They may create art that reflects historical themes, employs traditional artistic conventions, or seeks to convey a sense of timelessness and universality.

35. **(A)** Holi is a vibrant and joyous Hindu festival that is widely celebrated in many parts of India and by Hindu communities around the world. In Trinidad and Tobago, which has a significant population of Indo-Trinidadians who practice Hinduism, Holi is celebrated with enthusiasm and merriment. During Holi, participants gather together and engage in throwing and smearing coloured powders (known as "gulal") and spraying coloured water at each other. This playful activity is accompanied by music, dance, and festive food. The colourful celebration of Holi signifies the arrival of spring and the triumph of good over evil. The festival of Holi in Trinidad and Tobago not only serves as a religious celebration but also fosters unity, cultural preservation, and community bonding among the Hindu population and the wider society.

36. **(B)** The serpent, often depicted as the spirit or loa called "Damballa Wedo," is considered a powerful symbol in Haitian Vodou. Damballa Wedo is associated with creation, life force, and the primordial serpent. The serpent's presence represents the cosmic energy of fertility, rebirth, and renewal. In Vodou, the serpent is seen as a positive force and is associated with healing, transformation, and the cycle of life. It is believed to possess the power to bring forth new life, shed old skin, and initiate spiritual growth. The serpent's association with fertility and regeneration aligns with the beliefs and practices of Vodou, where the natural world and the spiritual realm intertwine.

37. **(C)** The plant commonly used to make baskets in the Caribbean is palm. Palm leaves or fronds are often used for basket weaving in the Caribbean. Various types of palm trees, such as the royal palm (Roystonea spp.) or the coconut palm (Cocos nucifera), provide long, flexible leaves that are well-suited for weaving. The leaves are typically dried, prepared, and then woven into intricate patterns to create baskets of different sizes and shapes. Palm leaf baskets are valued for their durability and strength, making them suitable for carrying and storing a variety of items. Basket weaving is an important traditional craft in many Caribbean cultures and has been practised for generations, serving functional, decorative, and cultural purposes.

38. **(B)** Cochineal is a natural dye derived from the dried bodies of female cochineal insects, specifically the species Dactylopius coccus. These insects are found on certain cacti in Central and South America. When crushed and processed, they yield a vibrant red dye that has been used for centuries. Cochineal dye is highly valued for its intense and long-lasting red colour, often referred to as "carmine" or "crimson." It has been widely used in various applications, including textiles, painting, food colouring, and cosmetics. The dye is known for its ability to create vivid red shades and is prized for its colourfastness. While other natural dyes like indigo (A), annatto (C), and henna (D) offer a range of colours, including blues, oranges, and browns, cochineal is particularly renowned for its ability to produce a bright and vibrant red hue.

39. **(B)** Colonial artefacts typically refer to items made or used by European colonizers during colonial rule in the Caribbean. During the period of European colonization in the Caribbean, which started in the 15th Century, European powers such as Spain, France, England, and the Netherlands established colonies in the region. These colonial powers brought with them their own cultural practices, traditions, and material goods, including various types of artefacts. Colonial artefacts can include

items such as tools, household objects, furniture, ceramics, weaponry, clothing, and religious objects that were made or used by European colonizers during the colonial period. These artefacts provide insights into the material culture and lifestyle of the colonial societies, reflecting the influence of European colonial powers on the local populations and the dynamics of the time.

40. (B) Edna Manley was a prominent Jamaican artist known for her contributions to modern and contemporary art. Manley's sculptures often explore themes related to Jamaican culture, identity, and social issues. Her works are characterized by a strong sense of realism and attention to detail, capturing the human form with expressive gestures and facial features. The sculpture "Beadseller" was Manley's first work in Jamaica. It was created in 1922 and depicts a woman selling beads. The sculpture marked a turning point in Manley's artistic journey as she transitioned from a European-influenced style to one that was deeply rooted in Jamaican culture. In many ways, her style evolved throughout her career, encompassing various influences and artistic movements. However, it is likely that her work incorporated elements of modernism, as she was active during the modernist period.

CAPE®

ART AND DESIGN

PRACTICE TEST 01

Paper 01

1 hour 30 minutes

READ THE FOLLOWING INSTRUCTIONS CAREFULLY.

1. This Practice Test consists of 40 items.

2. You will have 1 hour 30 minutes to answer them.

3. Each item in this Practice Test has four suggested answers lettered (A), (B), (C) and (D). Read each item and decide on the best choice. Look at the sample item below.

   Sample Item:

   The presence of cannons in the Caribbean is significant because they represent the region's history of

   (A) plantation slavery
   (B) colonialism
   (C) indentureship
   (D) buccaneering

   Sample Answer:

   The best answer to this item is "colonialism" and so (B) is shaded.

4. When you are told to begin, turn the page and work as quickly and as carefully as you can. If you cannot answer an item, go on to the next one and return to this item later.

RLF Publications.
"... redefining publishing..."

1. Which of the following accounts for the limited knowledge of Indigenous art and art forms in contemporary society?

(A) Indigenous people did not keep records of their art or art forms
(B) Indigenous people became extinct and their art forms did not survive
(C) Indigenous art and art forms were destroyed by European colonizers
(D) Indigenous art and art forms are difficult to understand or interpret

2. Which of the following European artists is known for his brightly coloured paintings of the rural and Indigenous life of Martinique?

(A) Isaac M. Belisario
(B) Adolphe Duperly
(C) Agostino Brunias
(D) Paul Gauguin

3. Which of the following items was NOT used by the Taino and Kalinago people up to the 1500s?

(A) Iron pots
(B) Stone pestles
(C) Wooden spears
(D) Ceramic bowls

4. Which of the following best captures parietal art?

(A) Cave art
(B) Performance art
(C) Kinetic art
(D) Indigenous art

5. Sfumato is a painting technique that is characterized by

(A) bold, contrasting colours
(B) soft, hazy transitions between tones and colours
(C) intricate details and fine lines
(D) strong emphasis on geometric shapes

6. All of the following music genres were created by Caribbean people directly in response to oppression EXCEPT

(A) Mento
(B) Reggae
(C) Calypso
(D) Chutney

7. All of the following Caribbean festivals are celebrated outside of the Caribbean EXCEPT

(A) Spicemas
(B) Caribana
(C) Carifiesta
(D) Labour Day Parade

8. In contemporary Caribbean society, the colonial architectural style is most commonly reflected in

(A) public buildings
(B) residential houses
(C) commercial buildings
(D) urban shanty towns

9. What was the purpose of the “Great House” on the plantations in the Caribbean up to the 1800s?

(A) Slave quarters
(B) Sugar processing
(C) Rum storage
(D) Owner’s residence

Items 10 to 13 refer to the diagram below which illustrates an architectural structure in pre-Columbian indigenous societies.

Source: https//en.wikipedia.org/wiki/Mesoamerican_pyramids (retrieved 30th November 2024).

10. The Indigenous groups that likely used the architectural structure in the diagram were

(A) Kalinago and Aztecs
(B) Aztecs and Mayans
(C) Taino and Arawaks
(D) Arawaks and Garifuna

11. The material that was primarily used to make the architectural structure is likely

(A) concrete
(B) limestone
(C) basalt
(D) stone

12. What was the primary use of the architectural structure?

(A) Historical archives
(B) Residential housing
(C) Religious ceremonies
(D) Recreational facilities

13. The technique used by the Indigenous people to create the depicted architectural structure was

(A) rammed earth
(B) wattle and daub
(C) lath and plaster
(D) layered mortar

14. What is the term for the way an artwork is arranged, or the way the elements are organized within it?

(A) Composition
(B) Contrast
(C) Balance
(D) Unity

15. Which of the following is a type of perspective that uses diagonal lines to create the illusion of depth?

(A) One-point perspective
(B) Two-point perspective
(C) Three-point perspective
(D) Isometric perspective

16. What is installation art?

(A) Art that can be carried in a pocket
(B) Art made with natural materials
(C) Art that is permanently attached to a wall
(D) Art that is created to transform a space

17. Naïve art is visual art that is

(A) created without any initial concept in the mind of the artists
(B) created by a person who lacks formal education and training in art
(C) not based on artistic techniques and perspectives
(D) derived from a distinct popular cultural context or traditional

18. The 1989 exhibition entitled "Les Magiciens de la Terre" was celebrated for its display and appreciation of

(A) African art
(B) Caribbean art
(C) European art
(D) Asian art

19. What is the term for the technique of creating images by assembling small pieces of stone or glass?

(A) Sculpting
(B) Mosaic
(C) Etching
(D) Engraving

20. What is the term for an artist who creates art with a focus on human emotion and experience?

(A) Emotionalist
(B) Expressionist
(C) Realist
(D) Romanticist

21. Which of the following is a common method of copyrighting works of art?

(A) Registering the artwork with the local government
(B) Stamping the artwork with a copyright symbol
(C) Posting the artwork online with a copyright notice
(D) Including a copyright notice on the artwork itself

22. Which of the following was a type of wooden carving found in the pre-Colombian Caribbean that was used in religious and spiritual practices?

(A) Zemi
(B) Calabash
(C) Guanin
(D) Santo

23. Which of the following is a key characteristic of Impressionist paintings?

(A) Precise and realistic brushwork
(B) Use of muted, subdued colours
(C) Depiction of everyday life and landscapes
(D) Emphasis on idealized and exaggerated forms

24. Which of the following BEST describes optical art?

(A) Abstract
(B) Expressionism
(C) Illusionism
(D) Surrealism

25. How have Adinkra symbols influenced Caribbean culture?

(A) They have become popular in music and dance
(B) They have been incorporated into visual art and fashion
(C) They have been used as inspiration for traditional festivals
(D) They have had no significant impact on Caribbean culture

26. Which of the following Caribbean islands is known for having the oldest Jewish cemetery in the Western hemisphere?

(A) Barbados
(B) Jamaica
(C) St. Kitts and Nevis
(D) St. Lucia

27. Which of the following is true of performance art?

(A) It only involves interpretative dancing
(B) It focuses on three-dimensional sculptures
(C) It is an art form that can be experienced live
(D) It utilizes digital technology and virtual reality

28. What is "wattle and daub"?

(A) A painting technique using wax and dye
(B) A building technique using sticks and mud
(C) A weaving technique using natural fibres
(D) A pottery technique using a special glaze

Items 29 to 32 refer to the photographic image below which reflects a mask-wearing event in the Caribbean.

Image used pursuant to the Creative Common License, retrieved from www.wikipedia.org (30th November 2024)

29. Which of the following Caribbean events is depicted in the photographic image?

(A) Vodou
(B) Junkanoo
(C) Kumina
(D) Pocomania

30. Which aspect of Caribbean culture is being celebrated in the depicted event?

(A) European
(B) African
(C) Asian
(D) Indigenous

31. The period that is typically associated with the cultural event is

(A) Christmas
(B) Easter
(C) New Years
(D) Ash Wednesday

---

32. Which of the following artists is known for a series of lithographs that depict the art form expressed in the image?

(A) Issac Belisario
(B) Phillip Wickstead
(C) Charles Robertson
(D) Agostino Brunias

33. UNESCO has confirmed many historical sites in the Caribbean. The acronym UNESCO stands for

(A) United Nations Education, Science and Cultural Organization
(B) United Nations Educational, Scientific and Cultural Organization
(C) United Nations Economic and Social Council
(D) United Nations Educational, Social and Commemoration Organization

---

34. The monument "Le Marron Inconnu" (The Unknown Maroon) was created to signify the freedom of enslaved people and is located in

(A) Martinique
(B) Guadeloupe
(C) Haiti
(D) Basse-Terre Island

35. Which of the following individuals founded the Working People's Art Class (WPAC) in Guyana?

(A) Aubrey Williams
(B) Stanley Greaves
(C) Edward Rupert Burrowes
(D) Donald Locke

36. Which is NOT a direct aim of the National Gallery of Jamaica?

(A) To promote Jamaican art
(B) To publicly display Jamaican art
(C) To preserve Jamaican art
(D) To market Jamaican art

37. The MAIN appeal of art movements in the Caribbean in the early 1900s was that they

(A) encouraged people to express their daily struggles through art
(B) promoted art as a meaningful career path
(C) encouraged the participation of all people despite socio-economic barriers
(D) focused on Afro-Caribbean customs and cultures

38. Which Hindu festival in the Caribbean celebrates the victory of light over darkness and is known for its vibrant display of oil lamps?

(A) Diwali
(B) Holi
(C) Navratri
(D) Durga Pujah

39. The oldest and largest public art museum in the Anglophone Caribbean is the

(A) National Gallery of Jamaica
(B) National Art Gallery of the Bahamas
(C) National Museum and Art Gallery (Trinidad)
(D) Museum of Antigua and Barbuda

40. Which of the following Caribbean artists are known for their artworks that reflect the vibrant and diverse artistic traditions of Haiti, including the distinctive style of Haitian Vodou-inspired paintings?

I. Hector Hyppolite
II. Wilfredo Lam
III. Philomé Obin
IV. Canute Caliste

(A) I and II
(B) I and III
(C) II and IV
(D) III and IV

ANSWER KEY FOR PRACTICE EXAM 01

Item No.	Answer Key
1.	C
2.	D
3.	A
4.	A
5.	B
6.	D
7.	A
8.	A
9.	D
10.	B
11.	B
12.	C
13.	D
14.	A
15.	B
16.	D
17.	B
18.	A
19.	B
20.	B

Item No.	Answer Key
21.	D
22.	A
23.	C
24.	C
25.	B
26.	A
27.	C
28.	B
29.	B
30.	B
31.	A
32.	A
33.	B
34.	C
35.	C
36.	D
37.	C
38.	A
39.	A
40.	B

EXPLANATIONS FOR ANSWERS FOR PRACTICE EXAM 01

1. **(C)** During the era of European colonization, there was often a disregard and devaluation of indigenous cultures and their artistic practices. European colonizers often imposed their own cultural values and norms, leading to the suppression, displacement, or destruction of indigenous art and art forms. Many valuable artefacts and cultural practices were lost or damaged as a result of colonization.

2. **(D)** Paul Gauguin, a French Post-Impressionist artist, is known for his paintings of Indigenous life and landscapes in various locations. In 1887, he spent time in Martinique and created a series of paintings inspired by the island's rural and indigenous life. His works from this period showcased vibrant colours and a unique portrayal of the local culture and landscape. The Paul Gauguin Interpretation Centre (Centre d'Interprétation Paul Gauguin) is located at Le Carbet in Martinique and is dedicated to famous French painter Paul Gaughin's stay on the island in 1887. He spent 6 months on the island and painted dozens of paintings during his stay.

3. **(A)** The Taino and Kalinago people did not use iron pots before the arrival of Europeans in the 15th Century. Iron and metalworking technologies were introduced to the Caribbean by the European colonizers. Before this time, the Taino and Kalinago relied on various other materials and tools for their daily activities. Stone pestles, wooden spears, and ceramic bowls were commonly used by these indigenous groups for grinding, hunting, and food preparation.

4. **(A)** Parietal art refers to art that is created on the walls or surfaces of caves or rock shelters. It typically includes paintings, drawings, or engravings made by ancient cultures on the interior walls of caves. These cave art representations often depict animals, human figures, and abstract symbols. Parietal art provides important insights into the lives, beliefs, and artistic expressions of prehistoric societies. The other options are different categories of artistic expression that may not specifically involve cave or rock art. Performance art (B) is a genre of contemporary art that involves live performances by artists. It can encompass a wide range of activities, such as theatrical performances, interactive installations, and happenings, where the artist's body and actions are the medium of expression. Kinetic art (C) is an art form that incorporates movement or suggests movement. It often involves the use of mechanical or technological elements to create dynamic and interactive artworks. Kinetic art can include sculptures, installations, and visual displays that utilize motion or optical effects to engage the viewer. Indigenous art (D) refers to the artistic traditions and practices of indigenous or native cultures around the world. It encompasses a wide range of artistic expressions, including visual arts, crafts, ceremonies, and rituals. Indigenous art reflects the cultural, spiritual, and historical experiences of indigenous communities and often incorporates traditional materials, techniques, and symbols. Indigenous art varies greatly across different cultures and regions.

5. **(B)** Sfumato is a painting technique commonly associated with the Renaissance artist Leonardo da Vinci. It involves creating soft, gradual transitions between tones and colours, resulting in a blurred or hazy effect. The technique is achieved by applying thin layers of translucent paint and blending them together, which creates a sense of depth and atmosphere in the artwork. Sfumato is often used to depict subtle gradations of light and shadow, as well as to create a sense of mystery and ambiguity in the composition.

6. **(D)** Mento (A), reggae (B), and calypso (D) are music genres that originated in the Caribbean and were created in response to various forms of oppression. Mento is a style of music that developed in Jamaica and has roots in African and European musical traditions. It emerged during the time of slavery and was a form of expression for the Jamaican people in the face of social and economic challenges. Reggae, also originating in Jamaica, arose in the late 1960s and became a prominent voice for social and political commentary. It emerged as a response to colonialism, poverty, and inequality, and played a significant role in promoting messages of unity, resistance, and empowerment. Calypso, primarily associated with Trinidad and Tobago, has its origins in the music and oral traditions of enslaved Africans. It developed as a means of social commentary and satire, addressing issues such as slavery, colonialism, and social injustices. Chutney (D), on the other hand, is a genre of music that is associated with the Indo-Caribbean communities of Trinidad and Tobago, Guyana, and Suriname.

This music genre was established as early as the 1940s within temples, wedding houses, and cane fields of the Indo-Caribbean. While it may incorporate elements of cultural identity and storytelling, it is not specifically linked to a response to oppression in the same way as mento, reggae, and calypso.

7. **(A)** Spicemas is an annual music and soca festival that takes place in Grenada. It is one of the largest festivals in the Caribbean and showcases a lineup of local and international artists. Spicemas is specifically celebrated within the Caribbean. On the other hand, the other options are celebrated outside of the Caribbean. Caribana (B) is a Caribbean carnival festival celebrated in Toronto, Canada. It is one of the largest Caribbean festivals outside of the Caribbean and features vibrant parades, music, dance, and cultural events. Carifiesta (D) is a Caribbean carnival celebration held in Montreal, Canada. It showcases the rich cultural diversity of the Caribbean through parades, music, costumes, and street parties. Labour Day Parade (D), also known as the West Indian American Day Carnival, is an annual event held in Brooklyn, New York. It is a vibrant celebration of Caribbean culture, featuring parades, music, dance, and traditional costumes. Collectively, these festivals are important cultural expressions that allow Caribbean diaspora communities to celebrate their heritage and share it with a wider audience outside of the Caribbean.

8. **(A)** In contemporary Caribbean society, colonial architectural style is most commonly reflected in public buildings. This is because public buildings often serve as symbols of power, authority, and governance, and they were designed to showcase the influence and presence of the colonial rulers during the colonial era. Public buildings such as government offices, courthouses, churches, and historic landmarks often exhibit architectural elements and designs influenced by European colonial styles, such as neoclassical, Georgian, or Victorian architecture. While residential houses and commercial buildings in the Caribbean may also display some colonial architectural influences, public buildings tend to be more prominent in reflecting the colonial architectural style due to their historical and cultural significance in representing the colonial legacy of the region.

9. **(D)** The purpose of the "Great House" on the plantations in the Caribbean up to the 1800s was primarily to serve as the residence of the plantation owner. The Great House was typically a large and impressive mansion or estate house that served as the central hub of the plantation. The plantation owner and their family would reside in the great house, overseeing the operations of the plantation and managing the enslaved labour force. The Great House often symbolized the wealth, power, and social status of the plantation owner, reflecting their position as the dominant figure in the plantation system. Additionally, the Great House was also used for various functions related to the plantation, such as conducting business transactions, hosting social events, and managing administrative affairs.

10. **(B)** The Indigenous groups that likely used the architectural structure of a pyramid were the Aztecs and the Mayans. Both of these Mesoamerican civilizations, which existed in what is now Mexico and parts of Central America, built impressive pyramids as part of their architectural and religious practices. The Aztecs, who flourished in the 14th to 16th Centuries, constructed large ceremonial centres with

pyramids as their focal points. One of the most famous examples is the Templo Mayor in the capital city of Tenochtitlan (present-day Mexico City). These pyramids served as sacred sites for religious rituals and ceremonies. Similarly, the Mayans, who thrived from around 2000 BCE to 1500 CE, built remarkable pyramid structures in their cities throughout the Yucatan Peninsula and Central America. These pyramids, such as the famous El Castillo in Chichen Itza, were used for religious and astronomical purposes and were often topped with temples or sanctuaries. The Taino, Arawaks, and Garifuna, were indigenous groups in the Caribbean and did not typically construct pyramids as part of their architectural tradition. Their architectural styles were characterized by simpler structures, such as round or rectangular buildings made from wood and thatch.

11. **(B)** The Maya and Aztec civilizations constructed impressive pyramids and other monumental structures using limestone and other locally available materials. Limestone is a sedimentary rock that is abundant in the region where the Maya and Aztec civilizations thrived, such as the Yucatan Peninsula and parts of Central America. It is a durable and relatively easy-to-work material that allowed the indigenous people to create intricate and monumental structures. They quarried limestone from nearby sources and shaped it into blocks or stones to construct their pyramids, temples, and other architectural features. The use of limestone in Maya architecture, in particular, is evident in famous sites like Chichen Itza. The smooth, pale appearance of limestone gives these structures a distinct visual appeal and has contributed to their preservation over centuries.

12. **(C)** The primary use of pyramids in various ancient civilizations, including the Maya and Aztec civilizations, was for religious ceremonies and rituals. Pyramids served as sacred spaces where religious activities, ceremonies, and rituals were conducted by priests and other members of the society. Pyramids were often associated with temples dedicated to deities and spirits. They were considered symbolic representations of the cosmos and were believed to be a connection between the earthly realm and the divine. The pyramids provided a platform for various religious practices, including offerings, sacrifices, prayers, and other ceremonial activities. Additionally, the layout and architectural features of the pyramids often incorporated sacred geometry and astronomical alignments, reflecting the spiritual and cosmological beliefs of indigenous people. They were designed to create a sense of awe and reverence, emphasizing the religious significance of the structures. Certainly, while pyramids may have had additional functions, such as serving as markers of power or symbols of social hierarchy, their primary purpose was to provide a sacred space for religious ceremonies and rituals within the ancient Maya and Aztec societies.

13. **(D)** The architectural structure of pyramids in Maya and Aztec societies was primarily made from limestone rocks layered with molten limestone. Indigenous builders used limestone extensively as the primary building material for their pyramids and other monumental structures. The construction process involved quarrying limestone blocks and shaping them into precise forms. These blocks were then layered and secured with mortar made from limestone mixed with water. The limestone blocks were carefully fitted together, creating a sturdy and enduring structure. The layered

construction technique and the use of molten limestone as mortar helped provide stability and structural integrity to the pyramids.

14. **(A)** Composition refers to the arrangement, placement, and organization of visual elements such as lines, shapes, colours, and textures within a work of art. It involves the overall design and structure of the artwork, including the relationships between different elements and their spatial distribution. Composition plays a crucial role in determining the visual impact and effectiveness of an artwork.

15. **(B)** The type of perspective that uses diagonal lines to create the illusion of depth is the two-point perspective. In two-point perspective, two vanishing points are used on the horizon line to create the illusion of depth in a two-dimensional artwork. The diagonal lines in the composition converge towards these vanishing points, creating a sense of space and three-dimensionality. This technique is often used to depict scenes with buildings or architectural elements, as it allows for a more realistic representation of depth and spatial relationships. One-point perspective (A) uses a single vanishing point, while three-point perspective (C) incorporates three vanishing points to achieve a similar effect. Isometric perspective (D), on the other hand, does not use vanishing points and maintains equal scale in all three dimensions.

16. **(D)** Installation art refers to an artistic practice where an entire space, such as a room, gallery, or outdoor area, is transformed or reimagined through the arrangement and placement of various elements, including objects, materials, light, sound, and other media. Unlike traditional art forms that are typically displayed on walls or pedestals, installation art engages with the viewer in a more immersive and experiential way. The artist creates an environment or an "installation" that is intended to evoke specific emotions, challenge perceptions, or communicate a particular concept or message. The installations often incorporate multiple sensory elements and can range from large-scale sculptural installations to interactive multimedia installations. The temporary nature of installation art allows artists to experiment with unconventional materials, engage with the surrounding architecture, and explore the relationship between the artwork and the viewer's physical experience within the space.

17. **(B)** Naïve art, also known as "primitive art" or "outsider art," refers to artworks created by individuals who have not received formal education or training in conventional art techniques and styles. Naïve artists often have little or no exposure to the established art world or its conventions. Instead, they rely on their innate creativity, personal experiences, and a unique perspective to create their artwork. Naïve art is characterized by its simplicity, childlike charm, and a lack of adherence to traditional artistic rules and perspectives. The artists typically depict subjects in a straightforward and direct manner, often emphasizing vibrant colours, bold outlines, and simplified forms. The artworks may feature naive or unsophisticated techniques, but they often possess a distinctive and authentic quality. Naïve art can be found in various cultures and is often rooted in specific popular cultural contexts or traditional practices. It celebrates the individuality, imagination, and personal expression of the artist, providing a fresh and unfiltered perspective on the world around them.

18. (A) The 1989 exhibition entitled "Les Magiciens de la terre" was celebrated for its display and appreciation of African art. It was a groundbreaking exhibition held at the Centre Pompidou and the Grande Halle de la Villette in Paris, France. It aimed to challenge the traditional Eurocentric perspective of the art world and expand the recognition of artists from non-Western cultures, particularly in Africa and other regions of the world. The exhibition showcased the works of both renowned and emerging artists, with a significant focus on contemporary African art. In doing so, it sought to bridge the gap between Western and non-Western art by bringing together artists from diverse backgrounds and cultures. It celebrated the artistic expression and creativity of African artists, shedding light on their unique perspectives, cultural heritage, and artistic practices.

19. (B) Mosaic is an art form that involves arranging and cementing small pieces of coloured stones, glass, or other materials to create patterns or images. The individual pieces, known as tesserae, are carefully placed and adhered to a surface such as a wall, floor, or object to form a larger composition. Mosaic art can be found in various cultures and time periods, with examples ranging from ancient Roman and Byzantine mosaics to contemporary works. The process of creating a mosaic involves selecting and cutting the materials into the desired shapes, arranging them according to the design, and then fixing them in place using an adhesive or mortar. Mosaics can be highly detailed and intricate, with the arrangement of the individual pieces producing a visually striking and cohesive image. The use of different colours and textures of the materials allows for the creation of depth, shading, and texture within the artwork. Mosaic art can be found in a wide range of applications, including murals, decorative panels, architectural embellishments, and even smaller-scale objects like jewellery and furniture.

20. (B) Expressionism is an art movement that emerged in the early 20th Century, primarily in Europe. It is characterized by a strong emphasis on expressing emotions, subjective experiences, and the inner world of the artist. Expressionist artists sought to convey their personal feelings and reactions to the world around them through their artwork. Expressionist art often features bold, distorted, and exaggerated forms, vivid colours, and dynamic brushwork. The artists may use these stylistic elements to convey a sense of urgency, intensity, or emotional turmoil. The subject matter of expressionist art can vary widely, but it often includes themes related to human emotions, social commentary, psychological states, and existential concerns. Expressionism is not limited to any specific medium or art form and can be found in painting, sculpture, printmaking, literature, theatre, and film. Notable expressionist artists include Edvard Munch, Egon Schiele, Wassily Kandinsky, and Ernst Ludwig Kirchner.

21. (D) While registering the artwork with the local government can provide additional legal protection and benefits, including a copyright notice on the artwork itself is a fundamental and widely recognized method of asserting copyright ownership. A copyright notice typically consists of the symbol © (the letter C inside a circle), followed by the year of first publication, and the name of the copyright owner. For example, "© 2023 John Smith." Including this notice on the artwork serves as a public declaration of the artist's rights and informs others that the work is protected by copyright. Posting the artwork online with a copyright notice or stamping the artwork with a copyright symbol can also be additional measures to assert copyright ownership and provide notice to others. However, including a copyright notice directly on the artwork itself is a common and easily recognizable method for asserting copyright protection.

22. **(A)** Zemis were carved wooden objects that held spiritual significance in the indigenous cultures of the Caribbean, particularly the Tanios. They represented deities, ancestors, or spirits and were used in various religious and ceremonial practices. Zemis took the form of anthropomorphic or zoomorphic figures and were believed to serve as intermediaries between humans and the spiritual realm. The other options are not wooden carvings used in religious and spiritual practices. A calabash (B) is a type of gourd that is often used for various purposes such as containers, musical instruments, and decorative items. Guanin (C) is an alloy made of copper, gold, and other metals that was used by the indigenous Taíno people of the Caribbean. It was primarily used for creating ceremonial objects and jewellery. A santo (D) is a carved and painted wooden statue depicting saints or religious figures in Latin American and Caribbean folk art. While they are associated with religious practices, they are more commonly found in the context of Catholicism and the syncretic religious traditions that developed in the region, rather than specifically pre-Columbian indigenous cultures.

23. **(C)** Impressionist paintings are characterized by their focus on capturing fleeting moments and impressions of everyday life. They often depict scenes from modern urban life, landscapes, and outdoor settings. Impressionist artists seek to capture the changing effects of light and atmosphere, using loose brushwork and quick, visible brushstrokes to convey their immediate impressions. Options (A), (B) and (D) are not defining characteristics of impressionist paintings. Impressionists are more concerned with capturing the essence and mood of a scene rather than depicting every detail precisely. They often employ vibrant and luminous colours to convey the effects of light and atmosphere. Furthermore, impressionists aim to capture the natural and unidealized aspects of their subjects, focusing on the transient qualities of light, colour, and atmosphere.

24. **(C)** Optical art, also known as Op art, is a style of visual art that uses optical illusions to create the impression of movement, vibration, or other visual effects. Artists working in this style often employ precise geometric patterns, repetition, and contrasting colours to create optical illusions that can deceive and confuse the viewer's perception. Op art aims to create visual experiences that engage the viewer and evoke sensations of movement or depth. The other options do not specifically relate to optical art. Abstract (A) is a broad term that refers to art that does not attempt to represent an accurate depiction of visual reality. While Op art can be abstract (A), not all abstract art falls under the category of optical art. Expressionism (B) is a style that emphasizes the expression of emotional or psychological states through distorted or exaggerated forms. Op art focuses more on visual effects and illusions rather than emotional expression. Surrealism (D) is a style that seeks to unlock the power of the unconscious mind and explore the realm of dreams and the irrational. While surrealism can incorporate elements of illusion or distortion, it is not specific to the techniques and visual effects associated with Op art.

25. (B) Adinkra symbols originated from the Akan people of Ghana and Ivory Coast in West Africa. These symbols hold cultural and philosophical meanings and were traditionally used to communicate messages and values. Over time, Adinkra symbols have spread beyond their original cultural context and have been embraced and incorporated into various aspects of Caribbean culture, particularly in visual art and fashion. In the Caribbean, Adinkra symbols have been adopted by artists and designers who incorporate them into their artwork, textiles, jewellery, and fashion designs. The symbols are often used to convey cultural heritage and identity and to express values such as wisdom, unity, and resilience. By integrating Adinkra symbols into their creative expressions, Caribbean artists and designers contribute to the preservation and promotion of African cultural influences in the region.

26. (A) Barbados has the oldest Jewish cemetery in the Western hemisphere. The cemetery, known as the Jewish Cemetery of Bridgetown, is located in the capital city of Bridgetown. It was established in the mid-17th Century and served as the burial ground for the Jewish community on the island. Barbados has a rich Jewish history dating back to the 17th Century when Sephardic Jews, primarily of Portuguese and Spanish descent, settled on the island. They played a significant role in the development of Barbados, particularly in the sugar industry. The Jewish Cemetery of Bridgetown is a testament to their presence and contributions. The cemetery is recognized as an important historical site and is visited by tourists and scholars interested in Jewish history in the Caribbean. It serves as a reminder of the diverse cultural heritage of Barbados and the lasting impact of its Jewish community.

27. (C) Performance art is an art form that involves the creation and presentation of artistic works through live performances. It encompasses a wide range of artistic practices, including but not limited to interpretative dancing. Performance art can involve elements of theatre, music, dance, spoken word, visual arts, and more. It often blurs the boundaries between different artistic disciplines. What sets performance art apart is its emphasis on the live presence and interaction between the artist and the audience. Performances can take place in traditional theatre settings, galleries, public spaces, or even unconventional locations. The audience experiences the artwork in real-time, witnessing the artist's actions, expressions, and movements as they unfold. Performance art can be highly experimental and may challenge traditional notions of art and artistic mediums. It can explore themes such as identity, politics, social issues, and personal experiences. The ephemeral nature of performance art, with its focus on the present moment and live experience, adds to its unique and dynamic qualities.

28. (B) Wattle and daub is a traditional building technique used for constructing walls. It involves creating a framework of woven wooden strips, known as wattle, which is then coated with a mixture of wet soil, clay, sand, animal dung, and straw, known as daub. This method has been used for thousands of years in various cultures around the world due to its simplicity, effectiveness, and the availability of materials. The wattle provides a strong structure, while the daub acts as an insulating and weatherproofing layer.

29. **(B)** Junkanoo is a vibrant and energetic street parade and festival often celebrated in the Bahamas, Jamaica and Belize. It is characterized by elaborate costumes, music, dance, and the use of masks. During Junkanoo, participants form groups or "shacks" and compete in various categories, showcasing their creativity, craftsmanship, and performance skills. The costumes are made from colourful fabrics, feathers, and other materials, and are often designed around specific themes or concepts. The masks worn by participants are an integral part of the costume, adding a sense of mystery and spectacle to the festivities. The masks can take various forms and designs, ranging from simple masks covering the face to more elaborate headpieces that extend beyond the head. They are often handcrafted and decorated with vibrant colours, patterns, and embellishments. The masks serve to conceal the identity of the performers and add a sense of theatricality and anonymity to the celebration. The other options reflect spiritual and religious practices in the Caribbean. Vodou (A) is a spiritual and religious practice that originated in Haiti. It incorporates elements of African religions, indigenous beliefs, and Catholicism. Kumina (C) is a religious and cultural practice primarily found in Jamaica. It has roots in African traditions, particularly from the Congo region. Pocomania (D) is a religious movement that emerged in Jamaica during the late 19th Century. It combines elements of Christianity, African spirituality, and ancestral worship. While ceremonies associated with these religions might involve mask-wearing, it is not a defining or typical feature as a whole.

30. **(B)** Junkanoo has its roots in African cultural traditions brought to the Caribbean by enslaved Africans. The festival features colourful costumes, music, dance, and elaborate handmade masks. The music is often played by a brass band or using traditional instruments such as drums, cowbells, and whistles. Junkanoo is a celebration of African heritage and is deeply connected to the cultural identity of the Caribbean.

31. **(A)** Junkanoo, also known as Jonkonnu or John Canoe, is a traditional Afro-Caribbean festival that is typically associated with the Christmas season. It is celebrated in several Caribbean countries, including Jamaica, Bahamas, and parts of Belize. The festival features colourful parades, music, dancing, and masquerade performances. Participants dress in elaborate costumes and masks, often depicting historical or mythical figures. Junkanoo has deep cultural and historical roots and is considered a significant part of Caribbean Christmas traditions.

32. **(A)** The artist known for the series of lithographs depicting the art form of Junkanoo is Isaac Belisario (1795-1849). "Sketches of Character" is a collection of lithographs by Isaac Mendes Belisario, a Jamaican artist of Jewish Portuguese descent. The series showcases scenes from Jamaican life, including the tradition of Junkanoo. Belisario's lithographs provide valuable insights into the cultural practices and costumes associated with Junkanoo. His painting and printing work also provide an eye-witness document of life in Jamaica during the period of emancipation.

33. **(B)** UNESCO stands for United Nations Educational, Scientific and Cultural Organization. It is an agency of the United Nations that was created in 1945 and aims to promote international collaboration in the fields of education, science, culture, and communication. It is responsible for designating and preserving important cultural and natural sites around the world, including historical sites in the Caribbean.

34. (C) The monument "Le Marron Inconnu" (The Unknown Maroon) is situated in Haiti's capital city, Port-au-Prince. It was created in 1967 by Haitian architect Albert Mangones and depicts in bronze a near-naked fugitive black man, kneeling on one knee, his torso arched, his opposite leg stretched back, and a broken chain on his left ankle. He holds a conch shell at his lips with his left hand, his head tilted upward to blow it, while the other hand holds a machete on the ground by his right ankle. The monument is regarded as a symbol of black liberation; commemorating in particular, the rallying cry that sparked the Haitian Revolution and the abolishment of slavery.

35. (C) Edward Rupert Burrowes (1903-1966) was a renowned Guyanese artist and educator who played a significant role in promoting and developing the visual arts in Guyana. He established the Working People's Art Class (WPAC) in 1948 as a platform for providing art education and fostering artistic expression among working-class individuals in Guyana. It aimed to make art accessible to all and played a vital role in shaping the art scene in Guyana.

36. (D) The National Gallery of Jamaica has multiple aims related to the promotion and preservation of Jamaican art. The gallery serves as a platform to showcase and celebrate Jamaican art, providing opportunities for artists to exhibit their works and engage with the public. It plays a significant role in supporting and promoting the development of Jamaican artists and their contributions. Additionally, the gallery also contributes to the preservation and conservation of Jamaican art, ensuring that it is accessible and appreciated by present and future generations. Marketing (D) is generally not an aim of the gallery.

37. (C) The main appeal of art movements in the Caribbean in the early 1900s was that they encouraged the participation of all Caribbean people despite socio-economic barriers. During this period, there was a growing emphasis on promoting art as a means of cultural expression and identity formation. Artists and intellectuals sought to involve people from diverse backgrounds and socioeconomic statuses in the creation and appreciation of art, challenging the notion that art was reserved for a privileged few. This inclusivity aimed to empower individuals and communities by recognizing their agency and providing a platform for their voices to be heard.

38. (A) The Hindu festival in the Caribbean that celebrates the victory of light over darkness and is known for its vibrant display of oil lamps is Diwali. Diwali, also known as the Festival of Lights, is a significant Hindu festival celebrated by Hindus worldwide, including in the Caribbean. It symbolizes the triumph of light over darkness, good over evil, and knowledge over ignorance. During Diwali, people light oil lamps called diyas to illuminate their homes and surroundings, create rangoli designs, exchange gifts, and participate in prayers and religious ceremonies. It is a joyous and colourful celebration that brings communities together to share in the festivities and cultural traditions.

39. **(A)** The oldest and largest public art museum in the Anglophone Caribbean is the National Gallery of Jamaica. The National Gallery of Jamaica, located in Kingston, Jamaica, was established in 1974. It houses an extensive collection of Jamaican art, including paintings, sculptures, photographs, and mixed-media works from various periods and art movements. The National Gallery of Jamaica plays a vital role in promoting and preserving Jamaican art and culture, showcasing the works of Jamaican artists and hosting exhibitions, educational programmes, and community events. It serves as a significant cultural institution and a hub for artistic expression in the Caribbean.

40. **(B)** Hector Hyppolite (I) and Philomé Obin (III) are both renowned Haitian artists known for their artworks that reflect the vibrant and diverse artistic traditions of Haiti, including the distinctive style of Haitian Vodou-inspired paintings. Hector Hyppolite (1894-1948) was a self-taught artist who gained recognition for his vivid and mystical paintings depicting scenes from Haitian folklore, Vodou spirits, and everyday life. His works are characterized by vibrant colours, intricate details, and a blend of realism and imaginative elements. Philomé Obin (1892-1986) was another influential Haitian artist who played a significant role in the development of Haitian art. He was known for his narrative paintings that depicted historical and cultural events, often infused with Vodou symbolism and references. His works capture the spirit and essence of Haitian life and history. Wilfredo Lam (II) (from Cuba) and Canute Caliste (IV) (from Grenada), although notable artists in their own right, are not specifically associated with the vibrant and diverse artistic traditions of Haiti and the Haitian Vodou-inspired paintings.

CAPE®

ART AND DESIGN

PRACTICE TEST 02

Paper 01

1 hour 30 minutes

READ THE FOLLOWING INSTRUCTIONS CAREFULLY.

1. This Practice Test consists of 40 items.

2. You will have 1 hour 30 minutes to answer them.

3. Each item in this Practice Test has four suggested answers lettered (A), (B), (C) and (D). Read each item and decide on the best choice. Look at the sample item below.

<u>Sample Item:</u>

What is a key feature of Gothic architecture in the Caribbean?

(A) Rounded arches
(B) Pointed arches
(C) Flat arches
(D) Shouldered arches

<u>Sample Answer:</u>

The best answer to this item is "Pointed arches" and so (B) is shaded.

4. When you are told to begin, turn the page and work as quickly and as carefully as you can. If you cannot answer an item, go on to the next one and return to this item later.

RLF Publications.
"... redefining publishing..."

1. Which of the following early forms of artistic expression was present in the Maya society?

I. Petroglyphs
II. Geoglyphs
III. Parietal art
IV. Hieroglyphics

(A) I and III only
(B) I and IV only
(C) II, III and IV only
(D) I, II, III and IV

2. Which of the following practices was closely associated with the religious practices of Neo-Indians in the Caribbean in the pre-Columbian area?

(A) Painting the body
(B) Smoking tobacco
(C) Sacrificing humans
(D) Slaughtering animals

3. Which is NOT a recurrent theme in Caribbean paintings?

(A) Landscapes and natural scenes
(B) Global wars and conflicts
(C) Syncretic religions and customs
(D) Plantation slavery and colonialism

4. Which of the following Caribbean countries have launched the "Paint the City" initiative which aims to rebrand its urban downtown area through the use of murals?

(A) Jamaica
(B) Barbados
(C) Grenada
(D) Guyana

5. Stephanie is a muralist. As part of her technique, she clears the wall and then affixes a painted artwork to the wall with adhesive. This technique is referred to as

(A) fresco
(B) graffiti
(C) mosaic
(D) marouflage

6. On what occasion is it likely for residents of Antigua and Barbuda to be wearing clothing made of madras textile?

(A) Independence Day
(B) National Dress Day
(C) Emancipation Day
(D) New Year's Day

7. Which of the following European artists is NOT known to have paintings or artworks based on Jamaican landscapes, people or festivals?

(A) Isaac M. Belisario
(B) Adolphe Duperly
(C) Agostino Brunias
(D) Camille Pissarro

8. How were the Cacique and Ouboutu similar in Indigenous societies?

(A) They were respected as elderly advisors
(B) They were leaders of Indigenous societies
(C) They were capable of communicating with the gods
(D) They were viewed as skilled craftsmen and artists

Items 9 to 11 refer to the intuitive painting below by a renowned Grenadian Caribbean artist.

"Racing Yacht" (1997). Image used pursuant to the Creative Commons Licence via Wikimedia, https://en.wikipedia.org (retrieved 30th November 2024)

9. Which of the following artists is likely responsible for the above painting?

(A) Phillip Moore
(B) Canute Caliste
(C) Hector Hyppolite
(D) Eva Wilkin

10. Which of the following is a likely feature of the body of work by the artist responsible for the painting?

(A) Use of precise lines and geometric shapes
(B) Vibrant colour palette and bold brushstrokes
(C) Realistic depictions of landscapes and portraits
(D) Minimalist approach with emphasis on negative space

11. In the context of the Caribbean, what symbolism is likely attached to the yacht in the painting?

(A) Freedom and liberation
(B) Migration and journeys
(C) Wealth and prosperity
(D) Healing and renewal

12. What are Adinkra symbols?

(A) West African proverbs
(B) Traditional dance movements
(C) Decorative patterns on textiles
(D) Carved wooden masks

13. According to the critical theory of art, the person with the most active role in the interpretation and engagement of the artwork is the

(A) maker of the art
(B) critics of the art
(C) viewer of the art
(D) owner of the art

14. Which of the following materials is the most commonly used in basketry making in the Caribbean?

(A) Bamboo
(B) Coconut
(C) Wood
(D) Straw

15. Which of the following architectural features is commonly found in Baroque-style buildings in the Caribbean?

(A) Gargoyles
(B) Minarets
(C) Buttresses
(D) Pediments

16. Which of the following is the oldest art organization in the Caribbean, founded in 1944?

(A) Jamaica Guild of Artists
(B) Art Society of Trinidad and Tobago
(C) Barbados Arts Council
(D) Puerto Rico Association of Artists

17. All of the following artists were instrumental in capturing Trinidadian society in the immediate aftermath of the emancipation of enslaved people EXCEPT

(A) Richard Bridgens
(B) Michel-Jean Cazabon
(C) Sybil Atteck
(D) Theodora Walter

18. Which of the following organizations hosts the annual International Caribbean Art Fair (ICAF) in New York City?

(A) Caribbean Artists Movement (CAM)
(B) Caribbean Cultural Centre African Diaspora Institute (CCCADI)
(C) Caribbean Art Society (CAS)
(D) Caribbean Museum Centre for the Arts (CMCA)

19. Which of the following hand-building techniques involves shaping clay by squeezing it with the fingers and thumb?

(A) Coiling
(B) Slab building
(C) Pinch pot
(D) Mould making

20. Which Caribbean festival is celebrated in Toronto, Canada, and features a parade, music, and food?

(A) J'Ouvert
(B) Caribana
(C) Reggae Sumfest
(D) Carnival

21. A copyright is

(A) the exclusive right to use and distribute a work of art
(B) the unique marks used to identify a piece of art
(C) the exclusive right to utilize a design in art
(D) the exclusive right to make, use, and sell an invention

22. Which of the following techniques is commonly used for creating small, intricate monuments that incorporate multiple materials?

(A) Collage
(B) Sculpting
(C) Welding
(D) Craving

23. What is the process of creating a monument out of clay called?

(A) Firing
(B) Glazing
(C) Sculpting
(D) Carving

Items 24 to 26 refer to the architectural structure below which is a mandir in Trinidad and Tobago to commemorate the arrival of Indian indentured labourers.

Image used pursuant to the Creative Commons License.
Source: https://commons.wikimedia.org/wiki/File:Waterloo_Temple,_Trinidad.jpg
(retrieved 30th November 2024)

24. What is the name of the mandir?

(A) Indian Caribbean Museum
(B) Temple in the Sea
(C) Dattatreya Mandir
(D) Saraswati Mandir

25. Which of the following explains why East Indians came to the Caribbean as indentured labourers?

(A) To provide cheap labour for the sugar industry
(B) To reduce the surplus population of India
(C) To demonstrate new techniques in sugar production
(D) To diversify the Caribbean population

26. The exterior of the mandir is white and light blue. What is the likely symbolism of this colour scheme of the mandir?

(A) Power and authority
(B) Love and compassion
(C) Purity and tranquillity
(D) Wealth and prosperity

---

27. What is the origin of Adinkra symbols?

(A) Kenya
(B) Ghana
(C) Nigeria
(D) Ethiopia

28. What material is often used as a primer for murals?

(A) Gesso
(B) Varnish
(C) Primer paint
(D) Stain

29. Which of the following materials is commonly used for creating a mosaic?

I. Ceramic
II. Marble
III. Stone
IV. Glass

(A) I and II
(B) I, III and IV
(C) II, III and IV
(D) I, II, III and IV

30. What is the process of obtaining dye from plant material called?

(A) Distillation
(B) Fermentation
(C) Mordanting
(D) Extraction

31. What is the name of the traditional method of tying and folding fabric before dyeing to create patterns?

(A) Batik
(B) Tie-dye
(C) Shibori
(D) Adire

32. Which of the following are NOT colonial artefacts in the Caribbean?

(A) Bohios and duhos
(B) Pottery and textiles
(C) Statues and sculptures
(D) Weapons and cannons

33. What is the role of "wattle" in a "wattle and daub" construction?

(A) To hold the structure together
(B) To provide insulation
(C) To create a smooth surface
(D) To add contour to the structure

34. What are some common features of Georgian architecture in the Caribbean?

(A) Arched windows and doors, intricate plasterwork, and spires
(B) Simple facades, minimal decoration, and clean lines
(C) Symmetrical facades, pediments, and decorative mouldings
(D) Rounded arches, stained glass windows, and flying buttresses

35. Kente cloth is known for its bright, bold colours and intricate patterns. What do the colours of Kente cloth traditionally represent?

(A) Royalty, power, and wealth
(B) Love, happiness, and peace
(C) The natural world, including animals and plants
(D) Religious and spiritual beliefs

36. What is a key characteristic of lithography prints?

(A) They are three-dimensional
(B) They are typically black and white
(C) They are only created using a brush
(D) They are created using a printing press

37. Collagraph is a

(A) digital airbrushing technique using graphic design software to remove blemished
(B) painting technique involving watercolours and ink layered on canvas or board
(C) painting technique in which paint is dabbed onto a surface using a bristle brush or sponge
(D) printmaking technique where materials are collaged onto a surface then inked and printed

Item 38 refers to the image below of porcelain (ceramic) dinnerware with underglaze flower decorations.

Image is in the public domain.
Source: https://en.wikipedia.org/wiki/Ceramic_glaze
(retrieved 30th November 2024)

38. Which is true of the underglaze flower decorations on the dinnerware?

(A) They were digitally airbrushed before the glazing and firing process
(B) They were hand-painted before the glazing and firing process
(C) They were engraved by laser after the glazing and firing process
(D) They were affixed by chemical reactions after the glazing and firing process

39. Which is a typical feature of Aztec art?

(A) Use of realistic and naturalistic representations
(B) Emphasis on abstract and geometric patterns
(C) Incorporation of intricate calligraphy and written language
(D) Depiction of serene landscapes and scenic beauty

40. Which is NOT a typical purpose of a mural?

(A) To commemorate a historical event
(B) To give political commentary
(C) To promote gentrification
(D) To beautify public spaces

END OF TEST

ANSWER KEY FOR PRACTICE EXAM 02

Item No.	Answer Key
1.	B
2.	B
3.	B
4.	A
5.	D
6.	B
7.	D
8.	B
9.	B
10.	B
11.	B
12.	C
13.	C
14.	D
15.	D
16.	B
17.	C
18.	B
19.	C
20.	B

Item No.	Answer Key
21.	A
22.	A
23.	C
24.	B
25.	A
26.	C
27.	B
28.	A
29.	D
30.	D
31.	C
32.	A
33.	A
34.	C
35.	A
36.	D
37.	D
38.	B
39.	B
40.	C

EXPLANATIONS FOR ANSWERS FOR PRACTICE EXAM 02

1. **(B)** Petroglyphs (I) and hieroglyphics (IV) were both present in the Maya society as early forms of artistic expression. Petroglyphs are rock carvings or engravings created by carving or incising images onto stone surfaces. The Maya civilization had a rich tradition of creating petroglyphs, which often depicted various subjects such as animals, humans, gods, and symbols. These petroglyphs served as a means of communication and artistic expression. Hieroglyphics refer to the system of writing used by the Maya civilization. It consisted of a combination of pictorial symbols and phonetic signs that represented sounds, words, and concepts. Maya hieroglyphics were intricately designed and adorned many artefacts, monuments, and murals. They served as a way to record historical events, convey religious beliefs, and communicate important information. Geoglyphs (II) and parietal art (III), on the other hand, are not specifically associated with the Maya civilization. Geoglyphs are large-scale designs or figures created on the ground's surface, typically using natural materials like rocks, gravel, or earth. Parietal art refers to cave art or paintings created on the walls or ceilings of caves.

2. **(B)** Smoking tobacco was closely associated with the religious practices of Neo-Indians such as the Taino and Kalinago in the Caribbean during the pre-Columbian era. Smoking tobacco held significant cultural and spiritual significance for these indigenous groups, and it was often used in religious ceremonies and rituals as a means of communication with the spiritual realm or as an offering to the spirits and deities. Painting the body (A) might have some religious significance, but it was an everyday practice for the Neo-Indians. Unlike the Indigenous people in South America and Central America, Neo-Indians in the Caribbean were not associated with human sacrifice (C). Slaughtering animals (D) has not been documented as a religious ritual in the pre-Columbian era.

3. **(B)** While various themes are depicted in Caribbean paintings, global wars and conflicts are not as prominent or recurrent compared to other themes such as landscapes and natural scenes (A), syncretic religions and customs (C), and plantation slavery and colonialism (D). Caribbean art often reflects the region's rich cultural heritage, history, and social realities, with a focus on topics such as Caribbean landscapes, local traditions, spiritual practices, and the legacy of colonization and slavery.

4. **(A)** The "Paint the City" initiative was launched in Kingston, Jamaica through the partnership of the Tourism Enhancement Fund, the Kingston and St. Andrew Municipal Corporation (KSMAC) and other organizations in 2021. It is a public art project and initiative aimed at revitalizing and rebranding urban spaces and promoting artistic expression through the use of murals and digital content. The "Paint the City" initiative has transformed the visual landscape of urban areas to create a vibrant and engaging environment for residents and visitors.

5. **(D)** Marouflage is a technique commonly used in mural painting where the artwork is created on a separate surface and then transferred or affixed to a wall or other support structure. The process typically involves preparing the wall by clearing any existing materials or debris and ensuring it is smooth and suitable for the attachment of the artwork. Once the wall is prepared, the painted artwork is carefully affixed to the wall using an adhesive or glue. The adhesive can be applied directly to the wall or the back of the artwork, depending on the specific materials and preferences of the artist. The artwork is then carefully positioned and secured to the wall, ensuring proper alignment and adherence. The purpose of marouflage is to create a durable and long-lasting mural that seamlessly integrates with the wall surface. By creating the artwork on a separate surface and then attaching it to the wall, the artist has more control over the painting process and can work on the artwork in a more comfortable and controlled environment. This technique also allows for easier maintenance and restoration of the mural in the future, as the artwork can be removed and replaced if necessary. The other techniques can be distinguished. Fresco (A) is a painting technique in which water-based pigments are applied to a wet plaster surface. The pigments bond with the wet plaster as it dries, creating a durable and long-lasting mural. Graffiti (B) is a form of visual art that involves writing, drawing, or painting on walls or other surfaces in public spaces. It is often associated with urban environments and is created using spray paint, markers, or other materials. Graffiti can range from simple tags to elaborate and intricate artwork. Mosaic (C) is a technique in which small pieces of coloured glass, stone, or other materials are arranged and set into a surface to create a pattern or image. The pieces, called tesserae, are typically square or rectangular and are arranged to form a larger composition. Mosaics can be used to create decorative and intricate artworks, often seen in architectural elements or as standalone art pieces.

6. **(B)** In 1981, Antigua and Barbuda became independent and chose the Madras textile as a symbol of their distinct identity. Madras fabric, characterized by vibrant plaid patterns, holds significant cultural and historical value in the Caribbean and is commonly used in traditional clothing. On National Dress Day, residents often wear traditional attire made of madras textiles to celebrate and showcase their cultural heritage. It is often draped as bunting on buildings and used.

7. **(D)** Camille Pissarro was a French Impressionist artist known for his landscapes and urban scenes in Europe, particularly in France. While he had a significant influence on the development of Impressionism, there is no record of him creating paintings or artworks based on Jamaican landscapes, people, or festivals. Instead, his artistic subjects were mainly derived from European landscapes and urban scenes. On the other hand, Isaac M. Belisario, Adolphe Duperly, and Agostino Brunias are European artists known to have created works inspired by Jamaican subjects. Isaac M. Belisario (A) was a Jamaican artist of Jewish Portuguese descent who is known for his series of lithographs titled "Sketches of Character" depicting scenes from Jamaican life, including street scenes, marketplaces, and portraits of individuals from different social backgrounds. Adolphe Duperly (B) was a French photographer who worked in Jamaica during the mid-19th Century. He documented Jamaican landscapes, architecture, and people through his photographs, capturing scenes of daily life, plantations, and notable landmarks. Agostino Brunias (C) was an Italian artist who

spent a significant portion of his career in the Caribbean, particularly islands such as Dominica and Jamaica. He is known for his paintings that depict scenes of everyday life in the Caribbean, including landscapes, plantation scenes, and portraits of Afro-Caribbean individuals.

8. **(B)** The Cacique and Ouboutu were similar in indigenous societies as they both served as leaders. The Cacique was a chief or leader in Taino societies. He held political and social authority within their communities, making important decisions and representing his people in interactions with other groups. He was also responsible for maintaining order, settling disputes, and organizing activities within the community. The Ouboutu, on the other hand, was a leader in the Kalinago societies. He held a position of authority and made all decisions, especially in times of war.

9. **(B)** The artist responsible for the painting “Racing Yacht” (1997) is Canute Caliste. Caliste is a renowned Grenadian Caribbean artist known for his intuitive and vibrant paintings. The other options are not associated with Grenada. Phillip Moore (A) is a Jamaican-born artist known for his vibrant and colourful paintings that depict scenes of Jamaican culture and landscapes. Hector Hyppolite (C) was a Haitian painter known for his naive or primitive style of painting. His works often depicted scenes from Haitian folklore, Vodou ceremonies, and everyday life in Haiti. Eva Wilkin (D) is an artist from St. Kitts and Nevis known for her colourful and abstract paintings.

10. **(B)** Canute Caliste is known for his expressive and colourful paintings that often feature bold brushwork and vibrant use of colours. His works often capture the energy and movement of Caribbean landscapes, festivals, and cultural scenes. Hence, based on the style commonly associated with Caliste, a likely feature of the painting is “vibrant colour palette and bold brushstrokes.”

11. **(B)** The Caribbean has a long history of migration, both voluntary and forced, which has shaped the cultural and social dynamics of the region. The yacht in the painting likely symbolizes the idea of migration, movement, and journeys, reflecting the experiences of Caribbean people travelling to and from the islands for various reasons, such as seeking opportunities, exploring new horizons, or reconnecting with their roots. It can also evoke the concept of exploration, adventure, and the interconnectedness of different Caribbean islands and cultures.

12. **(C)** Adinkra symbols are decorative patterns commonly found on textiles in West Africa, particularly in Ghana. They are visual symbols that represent concepts, proverbs, or messages. These symbols are often stamped or printed onto fabrics using carved calabash stamps and natural dyes. Adinkra symbols have a rich cultural and historical significance and are used to communicate ideas, values, and beliefs within West African societies. Each symbol has its own unique meaning and represents different concepts such as wisdom, courage, unity, and perseverance. Adinkra symbols are not only decorative but also serve as a form of visual communication and storytelling.

13. **(C)** According to the critical theory of art, the person with the most active role in the interpretation and engagement of the artwork is the viewer of the art. Critical theory emphasizes the importance of the viewer's subjective experience and interpretation of the artwork. It recognizes that the meaning and significance of art are not fixed or determined solely by the artist or the artwork itself but are co-constructed through the interaction between the artwork and the viewer. The viewer brings their own unique perspectives, cultural backgrounds, and personal experiences to the interpretation of the artwork, shaping its meaning and impact. Critical theory encourages active engagement, critical thinking, and dialogue between the viewer and the artwork, promoting a dynamic and participatory approach to art appreciation and understanding.

14. **(D)** Straw is commonly used in basketry making in the Caribbean. Basketry is a traditional craft that involves weaving or plaiting natural materials to create baskets, mats, and other woven objects. Straw, which is derived from dried plant stalks, is a popular material for basketry due to its flexibility, durability, and availability. In the Caribbean, various types of straw are used, including palm straw, sisal straw, and straw from other local plant sources. These straws are often harvested, processed, and then woven into intricate patterns and designs to create functional and decorative baskets. The use of straw in basketry reflects the region's rich cultural heritage and connection to the natural environment. Straw is usually created from the fronds of palm trees that grow in great abundance all over the Caribbean.

15. **(D)** Pediments are commonly found in Baroque-style buildings in the Caribbean. A pediment is a triangular gable that is typically located above the entrance or facade of a building. It is a distinctive feature of Baroque architecture and is often adorned with decorative elements such as sculptures, reliefs, or intricate carvings. The pediment serves as a focal point, adding grandeur and visual interest to the building's exterior. In the Caribbean, many historic buildings and landmarks, influenced by European architectural styles including Baroque, feature pediments as part of their design. The other options are not associated with Baroque architecture. Gargoyles (A) are decorative waterspouts, often in the form of grotesque or mythical creatures, that are commonly found in Gothic architecture. Minarets (B) are tall, slender towers usually associated with Islamic architecture, particularly mosques. Buttresses (C) are architectural supports or projections that provide additional structural stability to a building, particularly in Gothic architecture.

16. **(B)** The Art Society of Trinidad and Tobago is the oldest art organization in the Caribbean and was founded in 1943. It has been instrumental in promoting and showcasing the work of local artists, organizing exhibitions, workshops, and other art-related activities to support and develop the visual arts in Trinidad and Tobago, and even the Caribbean.

17. **(C)** In 1838, enslaved people in the Caribbean were fully emancipated. Richard Bridgens, Michel-Jean Cazabon, and Theodora Walter were all artists who were active during the immediate aftermath of the emancipation of enslaved people in Trinidad. They played a significant role in capturing and documenting the social and cultural landscape of Trinidad during that time. Richard Bridgens (1785–1846) (A)

was an English artist who arrived in Trinidad in the 19th Century. He created detailed sketches and watercolour paintings depicting various aspects of Trinidadian society, including scenes of everyday life, landscapes, and plantation scenes. Michel-Jean Cazabon (1813-1888) (B), born in Trinidad to a French father and Trinidadian mother, is considered one of the earliest professional artists in the Caribbean. He painted landscapes, portraits, and scenes of Trinidadian life, providing a valuable visual record of the post-emancipation period. Theodora Walter (1832-1914) (D), an artist from Trinidad, was known for her landscape paintings that depicted the natural beauty of the island. Her works often showcased the diverse flora and fauna of Trinidad, as well as scenes of rural life and village communities. While Sybil Atteck (1911-1975) (C) was a notable Trinidadian artist, she was active in the mid-20th Century and not during the immediate aftermath of the emancipation of slaves. Her artistic style focused more on abstraction and modernism rather than capturing specific historical periods or social contexts.

18. **(B)** The Caribbean Cultural Centre African Diaspora Institute (CCCADI) is an organization that promotes and celebrates Caribbean and African diaspora arts and culture. The organization is known for hosting the annual International Caribbean Art Fair (ICAF) in New York City. The fair provides a platform for Caribbean artists to showcase their works and for art enthusiasts to engage with and appreciate Caribbean art. The CCCADI also offers various programmes and exhibitions throughout the year to support and uplift Caribbean and African diaspora artists.

19. **(C)** Pinch pot is a hand-building technique in ceramics where the pot is formed by pinching and shaping the clay with fingers and thumbs. It involves taking a ball of clay and gradually pinching and shaping it to create the desired form. This technique is one of the simplest and most ancient methods of working with clay, and it allows for the creation of various vessel shapes such as bowls, cups, and small sculptures. Coiling (A) involves creating clay ropes and stacking them to build up the form, slab building (B) involves constructing forms from flat slabs of clay, and mould making (D) involves creating a mould to reproduce multiple copies of a form.

20. **(B)** Caribana is a Caribbean festival celebrated in Toronto, Canada. It is one of the largest Caribbean carnivals in North America and attracts thousands of participants and spectators each year. The festival features a vibrant parade, showcasing colourful costumes, energetic music, and lively dance performances. It is a celebration of Caribbean culture, music, and cuisine, with various events and activities taking place throughout the festival period. Caribana offers a rich cultural experience, highlighting the diverse traditions and heritage of the Caribbean community in Toronto.

21. **(A)** A copyright is a legal concept that grants the creator of an original work, such as a piece of art, the exclusive rights to use, reproduce, distribute, display, and perform the work. It protects the creator by giving them control over how their work is used and allowing them to financially benefit from their creation. With a copyright, the creator has the power to authorize or prohibit others from copying, reproducing, or distributing their artwork without their permission. Artists need to understand and protect their copyrights to ensure their creative works are used and credited appropriately.

22. **(A)** Collage is a technique commonly used for creating monuments that incorporate multiple materials. In art, a collage is created by combining various materials, such as photographs, printed images, fabric, text, and other found objects, and arranging them together to form a unified composition. This technique allows artists to explore different textures, colours, and forms by layering and juxtaposing different materials. When applied to monument creation, collage can be used to integrate various elements and materials, such as stones, metals, ceramics, and more, into a cohesive and visually striking artwork. It provides flexibility and versatility in combining different media to achieve the desired artistic expression. The other options can be distinguished. Sculpting (B) is the technique of creating three-dimensional artworks by shaping or carving materials such as clay, stone, wood, or metal. It involves removing or adding material to create a desired form or shape. Welding (C) is a technique used to join or fuse pieces of metal together using heat or pressure. It involves melting the edges of metal pieces and then bonding them together. Carving (D) is the process of cutting or shaping a material, such as wood, stone, or bone, by removing layers or parts of it with tools like chisels or knives.

23. **(C)** The process of creating a monument out of clay is called sculpting. Sculpting involves shaping and manipulating the clay to create a three-dimensional artwork. Artists use various techniques such as pinching, coiling, or slab building to mould the clay into the desired form. Sculpting allows artists to add details, textures, and intricate features to their clay sculptures. Once the sculpting process is complete, the clay sculpture may undergo further processes such as firing and glazing to achieve the desired final result.

24. **(B)** The mandir depicted in the image is the Temple in the Sea, officially known as the Sewdass Sadhu Shiva Mandir, which is a religious site located in Waterloo, Trinidad and Tobago. The temple was originally constructed by Sewdass Sadhu, a devout Hindu, in 1952. The Temple in the Sea Mandir holds historical significance because it was built by Sadhu as an act of devotion after facing challenges in finding a suitable location for a Hindu temple. Initially, he began building a small temple on the shore of the Gulf of Paria in Waterloo. However, his construction efforts were repeatedly dismantled and destroyed by the authorities who claimed it was illegal. Undeterred, Sadhu decided to build the temple in the sea itself to circumvent legal obstacles. He collected stones and other materials, carried them to the shoreline, and constructed the temple on a platform in the shallow waters of the Gulf of Paria. In contemporary times, the Temple in the Sea Mandir is a symbol of faith, resilience, and religious freedom. It attracts visitors and devotees from Trinidad and Tobago and around the world who come to worship, seek blessings, and learn about the remarkable story behind its creation. The temple also stands as a testament to the cultural and religious heritage of the Indo-Trinidadian community and serves as a significant landmark in the country.

25. **(A)** During the 19th and early 20th centuries, many Caribbean countries, particularly those with sugar plantations, faced a shortage of labour following the abolition of slavery. To address this labour shortage, plantation owners and colonial authorities turned to the system of indentured labour, recruiting workers from various regions, including India. The primary purpose of bringing East Indians to the Caribbean as

indentured labourers was to provide a cheap workforce for the sugar industry. Indentured labourers, often referred to as "coolies," were contracted to work on the plantations for a specified period. They were promised wages, housing, and other basic amenities in exchange for their labour. The recruitment of indentured labourers from India was also driven by economic factors. The sugar industry required a large and affordable workforce to cultivate and harvest the sugarcane crops. Plantation owners sought to maintain profitability by reducing labour costs, and the recruitment of Indian labourers provided a cheaper alternative to hiring European workers or continuing with the slave labour system.

26. **(C)** The likely symbolism of the white and light blue colour scheme of the mandir is purity and tranquillity. In many religious and cultural contexts, colours hold symbolic meanings. The specific symbolism of colours can vary across different cultures and religions, but in the case of the mandir, the white and light blue colour scheme is often associated with certain symbolic interpretations. White is commonly associated with purity, cleanliness, and spiritual enlightenment. It represents the absence of impurities and is often seen as a colour of sacredness and divine presence. In the context of the mandir, the white colour can symbolize the purity of the religious space, the spiritual aspirations of the devotees, and the quest for inner purity and enlightenment. Light blue, on the other hand, is often associated with tranquillity, peace, and spiritual serenity. It is a colour that evokes a sense of calmness and harmony. In the context of the mandir, the light blue colour can symbolize a peaceful and serene environment for worship and meditation, providing a space for devotees to find solace and connect with the divine.

27. **(B)** Adinkra symbols are a set of visual symbols or motifs that originated from the Akan people of Ghana. They are deeply rooted in the cultural and artistic traditions of the Akan, particularly the Asante and the Baule ethnic groups. These symbols have a rich history and are used extensively in various aspects of Akan culture, including clothing, textiles, pottery, and architecture. Adinkra symbols are often used to represent concepts, proverbs, and philosophical ideas. Each symbol carries its own meaning and represents a specific concept or value, such as wisdom, courage, unity, or beauty. These symbols are typically handcrafted and stamped onto fabric using a special dye made from the bark of the Adinkra tree, hence the name "Adinkra." In modern times, the symbols have gained recognition beyond Ghana and are appreciated for their artistic and symbolic significance. They have become popular not only in other African countries but also in the African diaspora and the global art and design communities. Adinkra symbols are celebrated for their beauty, cultural heritage, and the values they represent.

28. **(A)** Gesso is a traditional primer used in painting and mural making. It is a mixture of a binder, typically a combination of glue or acrylic polymer, and a white pigment such as chalk, gypsum, or titanium dioxide. Gesso is applied to the surface before painting to create a smooth, even, and absorbent surface for the paint to adhere to. In the context of murals, gesso is commonly used to prepare the wall or substrate for painting. It helps to seal the surface, prevent the paint from soaking into the wall, and provide a consistent base for the mural artwork. Gesso also helps to enhance the vibrancy and longevity of the paint. Before applying gesso, the wall or surface may need to be properly cleaned and prepared to ensure good adhesion. Once the gesso is applied and dried, the mural artist can then proceed with painting the mural using various paint mediums such as acrylics, oils, or spray paints.

29. (D) Items I, II, III and IV are materials commonly used for creating a mosaic. Mosaic art involves assembling small pieces of these materials, known as tesserae, to create a larger image or pattern. Each material has its unique qualities and aesthetic appeal, allowing artists to explore different textures, colours, and visual effects in their mosaic designs. Ceramic tiles (I) are a popular choice for mosaics due to their durability, wide range of colours, and versatility. They can be cut into various shapes and sizes, making them suitable for intricate mosaic compositions. Marble (II) is known for its elegant appearance and natural veining and adds a luxurious touch to mosaic artworks. Its smooth surface and variety of colours make it a sought-after material for creating detailed and visually striking mosaic designs. Stone (III), including materials like limestone, travertine, and granite, is often used for its natural beauty and durability. Stone tesserae can be polished or left in their natural state to achieve different effects in mosaic artworks. Glass (IV) is another commonly used material in mosaic art. Its vibrant colours and reflective qualities make it ideal for creating eye-catching mosaic designs. Glass tesserae can be transparent, opaque, or iridescent, allowing artists to play with light and create stunning visual effects in their mosaics. Overall, all of these materials (ceramic, marble, stone, and glass) provide artists with a wide range of options to explore and express their creativity.

30. (D) Extraction is the process of obtaining colour from plant materials by extracting the pigments through various methods. This typically involves soaking the plant material in a liquid, such as water or alcohol, to extract the dye compounds. The liquid absorbs the colour from the plant material, creating a dye solution. The specific extraction method may vary depending on the type of plant material and the desired outcome. Some common extraction techniques include simmering the plant material in water, macerating or grinding it to release the pigments, or using solvents to dissolve the colour compounds. After the extraction process, the resulting dye solution can be used directly for dyeing fibres or textiles, or it may undergo further processing or treatment, such as filtering or adjusting the pH, to enhance the dye's stability or colour intensity. Extraction of dyes from plant material has been practised for centuries and is a natural and sustainable way to obtain colour for various purposes, including textile dyeing, art, and craft projects, and traditional practices.

31. (C) Shibori is a Japanese textile dyeing technique that involves folding, twisting, and binding fabric before it is dyed. The fabric is manipulated using various methods such as tying with thread, stitching, pleating, or clamping with objects to create different resist patterns. These techniques prevent the dye from reaching certain areas of the fabric, resulting in unique and intricate patterns when the fabric is dyed. There are several different shibori techniques, including Itajime, Arashi, Kumo, and Nui, each producing distinct patterns. The choice of technique and the way the fabric is manipulated determine the final design. Shibori has a long history in Japanese culture and has been practised for centuries. It is known for its artistic and organic aesthetic, creating beautiful and one-of-a-kind patterns on textiles. The technique has also been adapted and incorporated into textile arts in other cultures around the world. The other options can be distinguished. Batik (A) is a traditional method of dyeing fabric that originated in Indonesia. It involves applying wax to the fabric in specific patterns and then dyeing the fabric. The wax acts as a resistor, preventing the dye from penetrating the areas covered with wax. After dyeing, the wax is removed, revealing the desired pattern. Tie-dye (B) is a technique that involves tying or folding fabric and then applying dyes to create vibrant, multicoloured patterns. The fabric is typically folded, twisted, or tied with strings or rubber bands to create different sections. The tied sections resist the dye, resulting in unique patterns when the fabric is dyed. Adire (D) is a textile dyeing technique that originated in Nigeria, particularly among the Yoruba people. It involves using cassava paste or starch as a resist to create patterns on fabric. The paste is applied to the fabric using various methods such as hand-painting, stencilling, or block printing. The fabric is then dyed, and the areas covered with the paste resist the dye, creating intricate patterns.

32. **(A)** Bohios and duhos are not colonial artefacts but rather pre-colonial Indigenous artefacts in the Caribbean. Bohios are traditional huts or dwellings constructed by Taino of the Caribbean before the arrival of European colonizers. They were typically made from natural materials such as palm leaves, wood, and thatch. Duhos were ceremonial stools or seats carved by the Taino of the Caribbean. They were used by the leaders or caciques as symbols of authority and power. On the other hand, options (B), (C), and (D) include various artefacts that can be associated with colonial influences in the Caribbean. The introduction of European ceramic techniques and materials, such as porcelain and stoneware, influenced the production of pottery (B) in the Caribbean during the colonial period. Textiles, including clothing and fabrics, also underwent changes and adaptations due to European influences. Additionally, colonial powers often commissioned and erected statues and sculptures (C) in the Caribbean to represent figures of historical and colonial significance, including monarchs, explorers, and military leaders. Lastly, the colonization of the Caribbean involved conflicts and wars, and as a result, weapons and cannons (D) were brought by the European colonizers and used during battles and fortifications.

33. **(A)** The role of “wattle” in a “wattle and daub” construction is to hold the structure together. The wattle, which is the woven framework of branches or twigs, provides the basic structure, and the “daub” is the material used to fill in the gaps between the wattle. The daub, which is typically a mixture of clay, mud, or earth, helps to hold the wattle in place and provide stability to the overall structure. It acts as a binder, ensuring that the wattle remains secure and forms a solid wall or partition.

34. **(C)** Georgian architecture in the Caribbean is characterized by several common features. These include symmetrical facades, meaning that the design elements on one side of the building are mirrored on the other side. Pediments, which are triangular or arched decorative elements, are often found above the main entrance or windows. They add a sense of grandeur and architectural interest. Decorative mouldings are another prominent feature of Georgian architecture in the Caribbean. These mouldings can include cornices, friezes, and window surrounds, among others. They are typically ornate and add visual interest to the exterior of the building. The other options are not associated with Georgian architecture. Arched windows and doors, intricate plasterwork, and spires (A) are more commonly associated with Gothic or

Renaissance architectural styles. Simple facades, minimal decoration, and clean lines (B) are characteristics of modern or minimalist architecture. Rounded arches, stained glass windows, and flying buttresses (D) are features often found in Gothic architecture.

35. (A) Traditionally, the colours of Kente cloth hold specific meanings in Ghanaian culture. Each colour is associated with certain qualities and symbolism. The bright and bold colours of Kente cloth are often used to convey messages and express social status. In particular, the colours red, gold/yellow, green, and black hold significant meanings. Red represents blood and is associated with vitality, spiritual strength, and sacrificial rites. It also signifies political and social power. Gold or yellow is considered a symbol of wealth, royalty, and prosperity. It represents the highest level of status and is associated with precious metals and the sun. Green symbolizes fertility, growth, and renewal. It represents the natural world, vegetation, and agriculture. Black is a symbol of spiritual strength and maturity. It represents the ancestors, the spiritual realm, and the collective history of the Ghanaian people. While love, happiness, and peace (B) are valued qualities, they are not traditionally associated with the specific colours of Kente cloth. The natural world, including animals and plants (C), is not directly represented in the colours of Kente cloth. Similarly, religious and spiritual beliefs (D) are not directly tied to the colours but may be expressed through the overall design and patterns of the cloth.

36. (D) Lithography is a printmaking technique that involves creating an image on a flat surface, typically a smooth stone or metal plate, using specialized drawing materials or ink. The key characteristic of lithography prints is that they are created using a printing press. Lithography prints can exhibit a wide range of colours and can be both black and white (B) or colour prints. While they can have a two-dimensional appearance, lithographs are not three-dimensional (A). Additionally, the creation of lithography prints does not exclusively involve the use of a brush (C); various drawing tools can be used to create the image on the stone or plate.

37. (D) A collagraph is a printmaking technique that involves creating a textured plate by collaging various materials onto a rigid surface, such as cardboard or wood. These materials can include fabric, string, leaves, sandpaper, or any other objects that add texture and dimension. Once the collage is complete, the entire surface is coated with a sealant to ensure the materials stay in place. After the sealant dries, the plate is inked, either by applying ink to the entire surface or selectively to specific areas. The inked plate is then pressed onto paper or another substrate, transferring the textured image. This process can be repeated to create multiple prints from the same collaged plate. Collagraphy allows for a wide range of textures and effects, making it a versatile and creative printmaking method. Each print can be unique, depending on how the plate is inked and printed, and the variety of materials used in the collage adds depth and interest to the final artwork.

38. (B) Porcelain is a highly durable and fine-grained ceramic material made by heating materials, typically including kaolin, to high temperatures, resulting in a white, translucent, and often intricately decorated product used in art, tableware, and industrial applications. The information provided is that the flower decorations on the dinnerware are “underglaze.” Underglaze is a technique in glazing and firing where designs are applied to the surface of a ceramic piece before it is covered with a transparent glaze and fired, resulting in vibrant, durable decorations that are protected by the final glaze layer. The typical method in decorating porcelain is to hand-paint the decoration before the glazing and firing process which allows the colours to fuse with the porcelain during the firing process. The other options are not typical ways to decorate porcelain.

39. (B) Aztec art is known for its emphasis on abstract and geometric patterns. The Aztecs had a rich artistic tradition that included various forms of visual expression, such as sculpture, painting, pottery, and textiles. In their artwork, they often used intricate geometric designs and abstract motifs, which were influenced by their cosmology, religious beliefs, and cultural practices. These geometric patterns were often symmetrical and repetitive, showcasing the Aztecs’ skill and precision in creating intricate designs. The use of abstract and geometric patterns in Aztec art was a way to convey symbolic meanings and represent the complex spiritual and natural world they believed in.

40. (C) While murals can serve various purposes, promoting gentrification is not typically one of them. Murals are often created to commemorate a historical event, celebrate cultural heritage, give political commentary, convey social messages, or beautify public spaces. They can be powerful tools for community engagement, public expression, and cultural preservation. However, the purpose of promoting gentrification, which typically involves the displacement of lower-income residents and the transformation of neighbourhoods for economic gain, is not inherent to the practice of creating murals. Murals are more commonly seen as a means of cultural enrichment, community empowerment, and creative expression.

CAPE®

ART AND DESIGN

PRACTICE TEST 03

Paper 01
1 hour 30 minutes

READ THE FOLLOWING INSTRUCTIONS CAREFULLY.

1. This Practice Test consists of 40 items.

2. You will have 1 hour 30 minutes to answer them.

3. Each item in this Practice Test has four suggested answers lettered (A), (B), (C) and (D). Read each item and decide on the best choice. Look at the sample item below.

Sample Item:

Which of the following art forms is most closely associated with the festival of Junkanoo?

(A) Face painting
(B) Mask-wearing
(C) Henna painting
(D) Lamp lighting

Sample Answer:

The best answer to this item is "mask-wearing" and so (B) is shaded.

4. When you are told to begin, turn the page and work as quickly and as carefully as you can. If you cannot answer an item, go on to the next one and return to this item later.

RLF Publications.
"... redefining publishing..."

1. Chiaroscuro refers to the technique of using

(A) multiple layers of paint to create texture
(B) bright and vibrant colours in a painting
(C) dramatic contrasts between light and dark areas
(D) symmetrical compositions in artworks

2. The colourful powder used during the Hindu festival of Holi, which is celebrated in some Caribbean countries, is called

(A) henna
(B) kumkuma
(C) mahavar
(D) gulal

3. The Art of Reggae Exhibition is an International Reggae Poster Contest that is displayed at which museum in Jamaica?

(A) The Bob Marley Museum
(B) The Devon House Mansion
(C) The Institute of Jamaica
(D) The National Gallery of Jamaica

4. Which of the following islands of the Caribbean Netherlands is known for its vibrant street murals and wall art in its capital city of Willemstad?

(A) Bonaire
(B) Aruba
(C) Curaçao
(D) Sint Maarten

5. The 2017 exhibition entitled "Circles and Circuits" by the California African American Museum (CAAM) featured Caribbean artists from Cuba, Jamaica and Trinidad and Tobago and was a tribute to

(A) African Caribbean art
(B) Hispanic Caribbean art
(C) Chinese Caribbean art
(D) Indian Caribbean art

6. Which of the following Caribbean cultural forms and expressions is generally associated with "*cultural resistance*"?

(A) Rastafari
(B) Carnival
(C) Calypso
(D) Vodou

7. Which does NOT illustrate the significance of Caribbean art forms?

(A) They indicate the historical experiences of Caribbean people
(B) They provide tangible expressions of the region's pride and identity
(C) They reflect the beliefs, values and attitudes of Caribbean people
(D) They showcase the colonial beliefs which remain in the region

8. A majority of contemporary Caribbean art forms are used to

(A) express socio-economic realities
(B) revive folklore and bring awareness to dying cultural patterns
(C) attract tourists and promote eco-tourism products
(D) strengthen regional unity

Items 9 to 12 refer to the image of Koo-Koo or Actor Boy by Jamaican artist Isaac M. Belisario.

Isaac Mendes Belisario, "Koo Koo, or Actor Boy" from "Sketches of Character, in Illustration of the Habits, Occupations, and Costume of the Negro Population in the Island of Jamaica, 1837-38"

9. Based on the image, what was the subject matter of Belisario, "*Sketches of Character*"?

(A) Plantation slavery and lifestyle
(B) Caribbean landscape and nature
(C) Carnival and masquerade customs
(D) Dancing and abstractions

10. What was the artistic technique used by Belisario to create the series?

(A) Layered oil painting
(B) Hand-painted lithography
(C) Palette paint brushing
(D) Woodblock printing

11. What is the MAIN inference of Koo-Koo or Actor Boy as depicted by the image?

(A) Blacks were seen as larger-than-life caricatures in the 1800s
(B) Blacks often combined African and European traditions
(C) Blacks expressed themselves through performance art
(D) Blacks used customs to represent African figures and deities

12. What method was likely used by Belisario in the creation of the series "Sketches of Characters"?

(A) Carving the images onto a block of wood
(B) Etching the image onto a metal plate
(C) Transferring the image onto a stone using greasy ink
(D) Painting the image directly onto a canvas

---

13. The Anse Cafard Slave Memorial which was completed in 1998 by Laurent Valere to commemorate the emancipation of the slaves in the French West Indies is located in

(A) Guadeloupe
(B) Martinique
(C) Saint Martin
(D) St. Barthelemy

14. Which of the following mythical creatures is a prominent figure in Caribbean folklore?

(A) Dragon
(B) Chupacabra
(C) Duppy
(D) Mermaid

15. What were the primary materials used in traditional indigenous Caribbean architecture?

(A) Wood and bamboo
(B) Stone and clay
(C) Grass and reeds
(D) Seashells and coral

16. Which of the following is NOT a construction method used in pottery?

(A) Pinching
(B) Slabbing
(C) Moulding
(D) Carving

17. What material are Adinkra symbols traditionally printed on?

(A) Canvas
(B) Silk
(C) Cotton
(D) Linen

18. What challenges might self-taught artists face in the art world?

I. Limited opportunities for formal exhibitions and shows
II. A lack of understanding of art history and theory
III. Difficulty in finding buyers for their work

(A) I and II
(B) I and III
(C) II and III
(D) I, II, and III

19. What is a midden in art?

(A) A type of sculptural installation
(B) A collection of objects and artefacts
(C) A type of painting technique
(D) A style of performance art

20. What is genre painting?

(A) A style of painting that depicts people in everyday life situations
(B) A type of painting that focuses on landscapes
(C) A form of painting that emphasizes religious themes
(D) A type of painting that portrays historical events

Item 21 refers to the image below which depicts an art piece called "Tree" by German artist Dennis Oppenheim.

Tree (From Alternative Landscape Components) by Dennis Oppenheim (2009), Schlosshof von Bad Homburg.
Source: https://commons.wikimedia.org/wiki/File:Blickachsen-7--23-dennis-oppenheim-hg-004.jpg (retrieved 30th November 2024)

21. The sculpture in the image is an example of

(A) optical art
(B) performance art
(C) installation art
(D) kinetic art

22. Which of the following Caribbean countries has the most recognized World Heritage Sites by UNESCO?

(A) Jamaica
(B) Puerto Rico
(C) Cuba
(D) Dominican Republic

23. Which of the following cultural groups contributed to the art form of mask-wearing in the Caribbean?

I. Europeans
II. Africans
III. Asians
IV. Indigenous people

(A) I and II
(B) II, III and IV
(C) III and IV
(D) I, II, III and IV

24. Realism is known for its focus on representing

(A) idealized and romanticized versions of reality
(B) surreal and dream-like images
(C) the inner emotions and feelings of the artist
(D) accurate and unembellished depictions of everyday life

25. Realism in the Caribbean was influenced by

(A) African art
(B) Indigenous art
(C) European art
(D) Asian art

26. What was the primary way enslaved Africans in the Caribbean maintained their cultural heritage?

(A) Through written records
(B) Through ceremonies and rituals
(C) Through formal education
(D) Through the adoption of European cultural practices

27. What is censorship in art?

(A) A process of reviewing and regulating art for public display
(B) A process of copying and reproducing art to a mass audience
(C) A process of preserving art in a museum for public display
(D) A process of determining which art is given attention by an audience

28. One of the limitations of using food to create art is that

(A) it is difficult to use food in art in the traditional sense
(B) it is open to various interpretations
(C) it is solely expressed in visual forms
(D) it is perishable and has a transient form

29. Which is NOT a function of the Institute of Jamaica?

(A) To compensate Jamaican artists for the unauthorized use of their work
(B) To establish and manage museums and galleries displaying Jamaican art
(C) To compile and publish artistic literature and data
(D) To maintain and display artefacts and art treasure

30. Which of the following mural techniques is often associated with inner city communities and is usually not sanctioned by official authorities?

(A) Fresco
(B) Graffiti
(C) Mosaic
(D) Marouflage

31. Which of the following art forms was associated with indigenous people in the Caribbean and Central America in the pre-Columbian era?

I. Engravings
II. Oil painting
III. Bronze casting
IV. Textile weaving

(A) I and IV
(B) II and IV
(C) II and III
(D) III and IV

32. A primary characteristic of intuitive art is that it

(A) focuses on realistic depictions of people, animals and objects
(B) captures emotions and feelings through various imagery
(C) uses geometric shapes and patterns
(D) is highly detailed with the corporation of text and written language

33. Which of the following hand-building techniques is commonly used in the creation of large vessels, such as water jars and storage containers?

(A) Pinch pot
(B) Slab building
(C) Coiling
(D) Mould making

Items 34 to 37 refer to the image below of an architectural structure located in the square of Bridgetown, Barbados.

National Heroes Square, Bridgetown Barbados.
Copyright owner unknown. Source: www.barbados.org (retrieved 30th Nov. 2024)

34. Which of the following BEST describes the architectural structure in the image?

(A) Cenotaph
(B) Gravestone
(C) Epitaph
(D) Memorial

35. Other than Barbados, which other Caribbean countries have similar architectural structures as that in the image?

I. Jamaica
II. Antigua and Barbuda
III. Trinidad
IV. Guyana

(A) I and III only
(B) I, II and III only
(C) I, II and IV only
(D) I, II, III and IV

36. Which of the following is being commemorated with the architectural structure depicted in the image?

(A) The arrival of the Windrush generation in England
(B) The death of Caribbean soldiers in World Wars I and II
(C) The emancipation of enslaved people
(D) The independence of Caribbean countries

37. Which of the following BEST reflects the symbolism of the architectural structure in art?

(A) The perpetual cycle of life and death
(B) The passage of time
(C) The connection between the living and the dead
(D) The celebration of cultural heritage

38. Which of the following landmarks in Jamaica has been operated as a house museum and is recognized as a National Heritage Site?

(A) Jamaica House
(B) King's House
(C) Devon House Mansion
(D) Vale Royal

39. Raffia weaving is generally associated with

(A) banana fibres
(B) palm fibres
(C) coconut fibres
(D) synthetic fibres

40. Which of the following styles of architecture is commonly associated with colonial buildings in the Caribbean?

(A) Brutalist
(B) Baroque
(C) Gothic
(D) Victorian

END OF TEST

ANSWER KEY FOR PRACTICE EXAM 03

Item No.	Answer Key
1.	C
2.	D
3.	D
4.	C
5.	C
6.	A
7.	D
8.	A
9.	C
10.	B
11.	B
12.	C
13.	B
14.	C
15.	A
16.	D
17.	C
18.	D
19.	B
20.	A

Item No.	Answer Key
21.	C
22.	C
23.	D
24.	D
25.	C
26.	B
27.	A
28.	D
29.	A
30.	B
31.	A
32.	B
33.	C
34.	A
35.	D
36.	B
37.	C
38.	C
39.	B
40.	B

EXPLANATIONS TO ANSWERS FOR PRACTICE EXAM 03

1. **(C)** Chiaroscuro is a technique commonly used in visual arts, particularly in painting, to create a sense of depth and three-dimensionality through the effective use of light and dark contrasts. It involves the skilful manipulation of light and shadow to create a strong contrast between illuminated areas and areas of darkness. This technique allows artists to create a sense of volume, form, and spatial depth in their artworks. By strategically placing highlights and shadows, artists can enhance the realism, drama, and visual impact of their compositions.

2. **(D)** Gulal is the colourful powder used during the Hindu festival of Holi, which is also celebrated in some Caribbean countries. Holi is a vibrant and joyous festival known as the "Festival of Colours." During the festivities, people playfully throw and smear gulal on each other, creating a lively and colourful atmosphere. The powder is made from a variety of natural and synthetic colours, and it is used to symbolize the arrival of spring and the victory of good over evil. Participants in the Holi festival enjoy dancing, singing, and chasing each other while playfully applying gulal on their faces and bodies. The other options can be distinguished. Henna (A), kumkuma (B) and mahavar (C) are dyes, powders and pastes used in Hindu cultural practices, but they are not specifically related to Holi.

3. **(D)** The Art of Reggae Exhibition, featuring the International Reggae Poster Contest (IRPC), is displayed at The National Gallery of Jamaica. The exhibition highlights the creative and artistic expressions inspired by reggae music and its impact on Jamaican and global culture. The gallery's role in hosting this exhibition aligns with its broader mission of promoting Jamaican art and culture.

4. **(C)** Curaçao, one of the islands of the Caribbean Netherlands, is known for its vibrant street murals and wall art in its capital city of Willemstad. The city is recognized for its colourful and artistic displays, with many buildings adorned with large-scale murals that depict various themes and reflect the local culture and history of the island. These murals have become an integral part of Curaçao's artistic and cultural landscape.

5. **(C)**The exhibition "Circles and Circuits" at the California African American Museum (CAAM) in 2017 specifically focused on showcasing the works of Caribbean artists from Cuba, Jamaica, and Trinidad and Tobago who have Chinese heritage. The exhibition highlighted the artistic contributions and cultural expressions of Chinese descendants in the Caribbean region. It also explored themes of identity, diaspora, and the intersections of Chinese and Caribbean cultures through various art forms, including painting, sculpture, photography, and multimedia installations.

6. **(A)** Rastafari is a cultural and religious movement that originated in Jamaica in the 1930s. It is often associated with cultural resistance due to its emphasis on African identity, liberation, and the rejection of oppressive systems. Rastas advocate for social justice, equality, and the empowerment of marginalized communities. Through their beliefs, music, art, and lifestyle, Rastas have used their cultural expressions as a means

of challenging colonial legacies, promoting self-determination, and asserting their cultural heritage. While Carnival (B), Calypso (C), and Vodou (D) are also significant cultural expressions in the Caribbean, Rastafari is particularly recognized for its role in cultural resistance and social transformation.

7. **(D)** Caribbean art forms are significant in many ways, but they do not generally showcase colonial beliefs that persist in the region. Instead, Caribbean art forms often reflect the historical experiences, beliefs, values, and attitudes of Caribbean people. They serve as tangible expressions of the region's pride and identity, representing the rich cultural heritage and diverse narratives of its inhabitants. Caribbean art forms can be a means of reclaiming and celebrating indigenous and African cultural influences, expressing resistance and resilience, and promoting cultural autonomy and self-expression. While colonial legacies may be referenced or critiqued in some artworks, the primary focus of Caribbean art is not to showcase or perpetuate colonial beliefs.

8. **(A)** Contemporary Caribbean art forms often serve as a means to express and explore the socio-economic realities of the region. Through various artistic mediums such as visual arts, music, dance, and literature, Caribbean artists address social, political, and economic issues that affect their communities. They use their art to comment on topics such as poverty, inequality, globalisation, postcolonialism, migration, and environmental challenges. These art forms can be powerful tools for social commentary, raising awareness, and initiating dialogue on pressing issues within Caribbean society. While other options like reviving folklore, promoting tourism, and strengthening regional unity may also be goals of some artists or art initiatives, expressing socio-economic realities is a fundamental and prevalent focus in contemporary Caribbean art.

9. **(C)** Based on the image, it is likely that the primary subject matter of Belisario's "Sketches of Character" is carnival and masquerade customs. Most of the prints that comprise "Sketches of Character" focused on different carnival and masquerade customs that were created by the enslaved people in the Caribbean. At the time, Belisario depicted individuals participating in carnival festivities and showcased the lively and spirited nature of this cultural event. At the time of creating these images, enslaved people in the Caribbean were on the verge of being fully emancipated. As such, it was a festive period. In modern times, carnival is a vibrant and festive celebration that is widely celebrated throughout the Caribbean region. It is characterized by colourful costumes, music, dance, and masquerade traditions.

10. **(B)** Belisario used the artistic technique of hand-painted lithography to create the series "Sketches of Character." Lithography is a printmaking technique that involves drawing or painting on a flat surface, usually a stone or metal plate, with a greasy or waxy medium. The image is then transferred onto paper using the principle that oil and water repel each other. In the case of hand-painted lithography, the artist applies the colours directly to the lithographic plate, creating unique and individualized prints. This technique allows for a high level of detail and vibrant colours in the final artwork.

11. (B) The image of Koo-Koo or Actor Boy represents a character that combines elements of African and European traditions. The costume and mask worn by the character feature African-inspired designs and symbols, while the overall theatrical presentation and performance style reflect European theatrical traditions. This suggests a fusion of cultural influences and a blending of African and European aesthetics and practices in the Caribbean in the early 1800s. This inference highlights the cultural syncretism and hybridity that is often found in Caribbean art and performance, reflecting the diverse historical and cultural influences in the region.

12. (C) Belisario used the method of hand-painted lithography in the creation of the series "Sketches of Characters." Hand-painted lithography involves the use of a lithographic stone or plate, which is a smooth surface typically made of limestone or metal. The image is drawn or painted onto the stone or plate using greasy ink or a special lithographic crayon. The greasy ink adheres to the drawn or painted areas, while the rest of the surface is dampened with water to repel the ink. When a paper is pressed against the stone or plate, the ink is transferred to the paper, creating a print of the image. In the case of Belisario's series, he likely created his sketches on lithographic stones or plates and then hand-painted the images onto the stones or plates using greasy ink or lithographic crayons. The hand-painted images would then be printed onto paper, resulting in the final lithographic prints. This technique allowed for the reproduction of the original drawings or paintings on a larger scale, making them more accessible and widely distributed.

13. (B) The Anse Cafard Slave Memorial (Mémorial de l'Anse Cafard), completed in 1998 by Laurent Valere, is located in Martinique, an overseas department of France in the Caribbean. The memorial is situated in Anse Cafard, a coastal area in the southern part of the island. It was erected to commemorate the history of slavery in the French West Indies and serves as a reminder of the struggle for emancipation. The memorial consists of 15 statues of stone figures, arranged in a triangular formation, looking out to sea.

14. (C) In Caribbean folklore, a duppy is a malevolent spirit or ghost. It is believed to be the soul of a deceased person who has not moved on to the afterlife or has unfinished business on Earth. Duppies are often associated with haunting, mischief, and the supernatural. They are prominent figures in Caribbean folktales, legends, and beliefs, and their stories have been passed down through generations in the region.

15. (A) The primary materials used in traditional indigenous Caribbean architecture were wood and bamboo. Wood was a readily available resource in the Caribbean, and indigenous peoples used it to construct their dwellings and other structures. They would often use large timber posts for the main framework and weave together smaller branches and palm leaves to form walls and roofs. Bamboo, another natural resource found in the Caribbean, was also used for construction purposes due to its strength and flexibility. These materials allowed for the construction of lightweight and durable structures that could withstand the Caribbean's tropical climate.

16. (D) Carving is not a common technique in the initial construction process of pottery. Instead, it is more commonly used as a decorative technique after the pottery has been formed using other methods. Carving can be done on the surface of the clay to create intricate patterns, textures, or designs. However, the primary construction methods in pottery are pinching (A), slabbing (B), and moulding (C). Pinching involves shaping the clay by hand using fingers and thumbs, slabbing involves rolling out flat sheets of clay and joining them together, and moulding involves using moulds to shape the clay into specific forms.

17. (C) Cotton fabric is commonly used as the base material for printing Adinkra symbols. The symbols are stamped onto the fabric using carved Adinkra stamps or screens made from calabash or wood. The fabric is then dyed using natural dyes, and the areas covered by the symbols resist the dye, creating a contrasting pattern. The resulting printed fabric is often used for clothing, accessories, and other decorative purposes.

18. (D) Items I, II and III are all challenges that self-taught artists might face in the art world. Self-taught artists may face challenges in gaining recognition and exposure in established art institutions and galleries (I). They may have limited access to exhibition spaces and opportunities, making it harder for them to showcase their work to a wider audience. Additionally, self-taught artists may not have had formal training in art history and theory (II), which can impact their understanding of artistic concepts, techniques, and contextual references. This can affect their ability to engage in critical discussions and navigate the art world's expectations and trends. Finally, without formal art education and established networks within the art world, self-taught artists may face challenges in finding buyers for their artwork (III). Building a reputation and establishing a market for their work can be more challenging without the support and connections that often come with formal art education.

19. (B) A midden is an archaeological term used to describe a deposit or accumulation of discarded materials, such as shells, bones, tools, and other artefacts, that provides insights into past human activities and culture. In art, the term "midden" may be used to describe an assemblage or installation of objects or materials, often arranged in a deliberate or meaningful way, to create a visual composition or convey a particular concept or message. It can be a form of artistic expression that explores the relationships between objects, materials, and cultural meanings.

20. (A) Genre painting refers to a style of painting that depicts people in everyday life situations. It often portrays scenes from ordinary life, domestic settings, social gatherings, or mundane activities. Genre paintings aim to capture the customs, behaviours, and atmosphere of a particular time period or social context. These works of art can provide insights into the daily lives, values, and cultural practices of the people depicted. The subjects of genre paintings can vary widely, including depictions of peasants, merchants, families, street scenes, interiors, and more. The focus is on capturing the essence of everyday life rather than grand historical or religious narratives.

21. (C) The image reflects a notable installation artwork created by Dennis Oppenheim entitled "Tree." Installation art is a contemporary art form that involves creating immersive, three-dimensional environments or installations in a specific space. It goes beyond traditional two-dimensional artwork such as paintings or sculptures and instead uses various materials, objects, sound, light, and other elements to transform the viewer's perception and experience of the space. Installation art often takes into account the architectural, spatial, and environmental aspects of the exhibition space, utilizing the entire area as a canvas for artistic expression. The artist may arrange objects, construct structures, incorporate multimedia elements, or manipulate the space itself to create a unique and immersive environment. Installations can be site-specific, meaning they are designed specifically for a particular location, or they can be reconfigured and adapted to different spaces. The specific artwork in the image invites viewers to question their assumptions about the natural world and the constructed environment, blurring the boundaries between the two. "Tree" is an example of how installation art can provoke contemplation and stimulate dialogue about our relationship with nature and the broader concepts of art and representation.

22. (C) The Caribbean country with the most recognized World Heritage Sites by UNESCO is Cuba. Cuba boasts a rich cultural and historical heritage, which has earned it multiple UNESCO World Heritage Site designations. To date, Cuba has a total of nine World Heritage Sites, which include Old Havana and its Fortification System, Trinidad and the Valley de los Ingenios, Viñales Valley, and the Historic Center of Cienfuegos, among others.

23. (D) Items I, II, III and IV are all cultural groups that have contributed to the art form of mask-wearing in the Caribbean. Each cultural group has brought its own unique traditions, beliefs, and artistic expressions to the region, including the creation and use of masks. These masks may serve various purposes, such as ceremonial or religious practices, storytelling, cultural performances, and masquerade traditions. The specific styles, materials, and designs of the masks can vary based on the cultural influences and historical context of each group.

24. (D) Realism is an art movement that emerged in the mid-19th Century as a reaction against the idealized and romanticized depictions of the previous art movements. Realist artists aimed to represent the world as it is, without romanticizing or idealizing it. They focused on portraying the ordinary, everyday life of common people, often depicting scenes from urban or rural settings, labourers, and ordinary objects. Realism sought to capture the truth and authenticity of reality through careful observation and meticulous attention to detail. The goal was to provide an objective and faithful representation of the world, free from the influence of personal emotions or subjective interpretations.

25. (C) Realism in the Caribbean was influenced by European art. During the colonial period, European artistic styles and techniques were introduced to the Caribbean through colonization and trade. European artists, particularly those from France, Spain, England, and the Netherlands had a significant impact on the development of art in the Caribbean. Their artistic traditions, including the realist approach, were assimilated and adapted by Caribbean artists. Caribbean artists who studied or travelled to Europe were exposed to European art movements, such as Realism, and incorporated those influences into their work. They adopted the principles of representing everyday life and depicting subjects with accuracy and detail. However, it is important to note that Caribbean artists also infused their own cultural perspectives and experiences into their artistic expressions, resulting in a unique blend of European influence and Caribbean sensibilities.

26. **(B)** The primary way enslaved Africans in the Caribbean maintained their cultural heritage was through private ceremonies and rituals. Enslaved Africans in the Caribbean faced immense challenges in preserving their cultural heritage due to the oppressive conditions of slavery. However, they found ways to maintain their cultural traditions and pass them down through generations. One of the most significant ways they did this was through the preservation and practice of their traditional ceremonies and rituals. These ceremonies and rituals provided a space for enslaved Africans to express their cultural identity, celebrate their ancestral customs, and maintain a sense of community and belonging. They encompassed various aspects of African culture, including music, dance, storytelling, religious practices, and healing traditions. Through these communal gatherings and performances, enslaved Africans were able to connect with their African roots, transmit their cultural knowledge, and keep their traditions alive in the face of adversity. Written records (A) were not accessible to most enslaved Africans, as their literacy was often discouraged or prohibited by slave owners. Formal education (C) was generally denied to enslaved Africans, as it was seen as a means of empowerment and potential rebellion. While some enslaved Africans may have adopted certain European cultural practices (D) for survival or assimilation purposes, it was not the primary way they maintained their cultural heritage.

27. **(A)** Censorship in art refers to the process of reviewing and regulating art for public display. It involves the suppression, restriction, or control of artistic expression, often by governmental or institutional authorities. Censorship can take various forms, including the removal, alteration, or prohibition of artwork deemed offensive, controversial, or inappropriate according to certain standards or ideologies. The purpose of art censorship can vary depending on the context and the intentions of the censors. It may be driven by concerns over political dissent, religious sensitivities, moral values, obscenity, or the preservation of social order. Censorship in art has been practised throughout history in different societies and under different political systems. Art censorship raises significant ethical and philosophical questions regarding freedom of expression, creativity, and the role of art in society. It can have a profound impact on artists, limiting their ability to convey certain ideas, challenge established norms, or express dissenting viewpoints. At the same time, proponents of censorship argue that it is necessary to maintain social harmony, protect public morals, or prevent the dissemination of harmful or offensive content. The balance between artistic freedom and censorship is a complex and ongoing debate in the art world.

28. **(D)** One of the limitations of using food to create art is that it is perishable and has a transient form. Food is organic and subject to decay, spoilage, and changes in appearance, texture, and smell over time. This makes it challenging to create long-lasting and permanent artworks using food as the primary medium. Unlike more durable artistic materials such as paint, clay, or metal, food artworks have a limited lifespan and are often intended to be consumed or discarded after a certain period. The temporary nature of food art can pose challenges for preservation, exhibition, and documentation. While the ephemerality of food art can be seen as part of its appeal, allowing viewers to experience the artwork in a unique and time-bound way, it also means that the artistic expression and impact may be short-lived. Documentation through photography or video recording becomes crucial to capture and share the artwork beyond its immediate presence. Additionally, the perishable nature of food limits the scale, complexity, and transportation of food art. It may be difficult to create intricate or large-scale artworks using food materials, as they may be prone to deterioration or require specialized preservation techniques. Despite these limitations, artists have embraced the use of food as a medium for its sensory and symbolic qualities, exploring themes of consumption, identity, culture, and sustainability. Food art challenges traditional notions of artistic permanence and invites viewers to engage with art in a multisensory and thought-provoking way.

29. **(A)** The Institute of Jamaica, based in Kingston, Jamaica, is a cultural organization that plays a significant role in the preservation, promotion, and development of Jamaican art, culture, and heritage. Options (B), (C) and (D) are all functions of the Institute of Jamaica. Additionally, the Institute also promotes educational programmes, supports artistic and cultural initiatives, organizes exhibitions, and fosters collaboration and exchange in the arts and culture sector. Compensating Jamaican artists for the unauthorized use of their work is not a function of the Institute of Jamaica.

30. **(B)** Graffiti is a mural technique that is often associated with inner-city communities and is typically not sanctioned by official authorities. It involves the use of spray paint or other marking materials to create artistic designs or writings on public walls, surfaces, or structures. Graffiti is known for its vibrant colours and intricate lettering styles, and often serves as a form of self-expression or political commentary. While graffiti can be seen as an act of vandalism when done without permission, it has also gained recognition as a legitimate art form and has been embraced in certain contexts, such as street art festivals or designated graffiti zones.

31. **(A)** Engravings (I) and textile weaving (IV) were art forms associated with indigenous people in the Caribbean and Central America in the pre-Columbian era. Engravings were often created on various materials such as stone, bone, or shell, and depicted intricate patterns, symbols, or scenes that held cultural and religious significance. Textile weaving was also a prominent art form, where Indigenous people used natural fibres such as cotton or agave to create elaborate textiles with intricate designs and patterns. These art forms reflected the rich cultural heritage and artistic traditions of the Indigenous populations in the region. Oil painting (II) and bronze casting (III), on the other hand, were introduced to the Americas after the arrival of European colonizers.

32. **(B)** Intuitive art, also known as "art brut" or "outsider art," is characterized by its spontaneous and uninhibited nature. It is often created by self-taught artists who have little or no formal training in art techniques and may not adhere to conventional artistic standards. One of the primary characteristics of intuitive art is its ability to convey emotions and feelings through the use of imagery. Artists express their inner thoughts, experiences, and perspectives through their artwork, often using symbolism, expressive brushwork, vibrant colours, and abstract or fantastical elements. Intuitive art is deeply personal and can provide a direct and unfiltered expression of the artist's emotions and experiences.

33. **(C)** Coiling is a hand-building technique in pottery where long coils of clay are rolled and stacked on top of each other to create the desired form. This method is commonly used in the creation of large vessels such as water jars and storage containers. The coils are joined together by blending or scoring the clay surfaces, creating a strong bond. The process allows for the gradual building up of the form and provides flexibility in shaping and adding details. Coiling is an ancient technique that has been used by various cultures throughout history to create functional and decorative pottery.

34. **(A)** The architectural structure in the image is a cenotaph which is a type of monument that is built in honour of a person or group of people who are buried elsewhere or whose remains are not present at the site. Cenotaphs are typically erected as memorials to commemorate individuals who have died, particularly those who have made significant contributions or sacrifices. They can take various forms, including statues, pillars, obelisks, or architectural structures, and are often located in public spaces such as parks, squares, or cemeteries, serving as focal points for remembrance and commemoration. Unlike a traditional tomb or burial site, a cenotaph does not contain the physical remains of the person or people it commemorates. Instead, it serves as a symbolic representation and reminder of their memory, achievements, or the significance of their contributions. Cenotaphs can be found throughout the Caribbean.

35. **(D)** Cenotaphs are found throughout the Caribbean with some notable ones being in Jamaica (I), Antigua and Barbuda (II), Trinidad (III) and Guyana (IV). The National Heroes Park in Kingston, Jamaica, is home to a cenotaph known as the National Heroes Monument. It commemorates Jamaica's national heroes and prominent figures. The cenotaph in Antigua and Barbuda is located in the capital city, St. John's. It stands in the Botanical Gardens and serves as a memorial to the Antiguan and Barbudan soldiers who lost their lives in World War I and World War II. In Trinidad and Tobago, a cenotaph is situated in Memorial Park, Port of Spain. This cenotaph serves as a memorial for soldiers who died in World Wars I and II, as well as other military conflicts. Guyana's cenotaph is located in Georgetown, the capital city. It stands in the Georgetown Botanical Gardens and commemorates the soldiers from Guyana who died in various wars and conflicts.

36. (B) Most cenotaphs in the Caribbean, as in other parts of the world, were erected to honour and remember the soldiers who lost their lives in World Wars I and II. These cenotaphs serve as memorials and symbols of remembrance for the sacrifices made by the soldiers from the Caribbean region during these conflicts. They are important commemorative structures that pay tribute to the fallen soldiers and their contributions to the war efforts.

37. (C) Architecture often serves as a physical representation of the human experience and can symbolize various aspects of life and culture. Additionally, architectural structures can have artistic interpretations. A cenotaph is a monument erected in memory of a person whose body is elsewhere. In the context of art, it generally reflects the connection between the living and the dead. Indeed, it serves as a symbolic resting place and a focal point for remembrance, thus bridging the gap between the living and the deceased. It can also represent themes of spirituality, ancestral heritage, or the continuity of life beyond death.

38. (C) The Devon House Mansion, located in Kingston, Jamaica, is a historic mansion that was built in the late 19th century. It was the residence of George Stiebel, Jamaica's first black millionaire. Today, Devon House Mansion is operated as a house museum and offers visitors a glimpse into the rich history and culture of Jamaica. It is known for its well-preserved Georgian architecture, beautiful gardens, and its significance as a symbol of Jamaican heritage.

39. (B) Raffia is a type of fibre that is obtained from the leaves of the raffia palm tree (Raphia spp.). The leaves are stripped to extract the long fibres, which are then dried and used for weaving. Raffia weaving is a traditional craft that has been practised in various cultures, particularly in Africa. The flexible and durable nature of raffia fibres makes them suitable for creating a wide range of woven products, including baskets, mats, hats, and decorative items. The natural colour and texture of raffia fibres contribute to the unique and organic aesthetic of raffia weaving.

40. (B) The style of architecture commonly associated with colonial buildings in the Caribbean is baroque. Indeed, baroque architecture was prevalent during the colonial period in the Caribbean, particularly during the 17th and 18th centuries. It is characterized by elaborate ornamentation, grandeur, and dramatic elements. Baroque architecture features intricate detailing, curved forms, decorative motifs, and a sense of movement. It often includes elements such as domes, columns, pilasters, and ornate facades. This architectural style was influenced by European Baroque architecture and was adopted by the colonial powers in their construction of churches, government buildings, and grand residences in the Caribbean. The Baroque style reflected the power, wealth, and influence of the colonial rulers during that time.

CAPE®

ART AND DESIGN

PRACTICE TEST 04

Paper 01

1 hour 30 minutes

READ THE FOLLOWING INSTRUCTIONS CAREFULLY.

1. This Practice Test consists of 40 items.

2. You will have 1 hour 30 minutes to answer them.

3. Each item in this Practice Test has four suggested answers lettered (A), (B), (C) and (D). Read each item and decide on the best choice. Look at the sample item below.

   Sample Item:

   Which Trinidadian artist is known for his extravagant and innovative designs for the Olympic Games of 1992 and 1996?

   (A) Sybil Atteck
   (B) Peter Minshall
   (C) Esther Griffiths
   (D) Boschoe Holder

   Sample Answer:

   The best answer to this item is “Peter Minshall” and so (B) is shaded.

4. When you are told to begin, turn the page and work as quickly and as carefully as you can. If you cannot answer an item, go on to the next one and return to this item later.

RLF Publications.
"... redefining publishing..."

Items 1 to 4 refer to the image below which represents architectural structures in Caribbean indigenous societies up to the 1500s.

Depiction of Indigenous houses by Gonzalo Fernández de Oviedo, Crónica de las Indias, Salamanca, 1547. Source: https://www.floridamuseum.ufl.edu/histarch/research/haiti/en-bas-saline/taino-society/ (retrieved 30th November 2024)

1. Which of the following Indigenous groups did NOT use these architectural structures for shelter?

(A) Maya
(B) Taino
(C) Ciboney
(D) Garifuna

2. What names BEST describe these architectural structures?

(A) Bohio and caney
(B) Carbet and hut
(C) Temple and mandir
(D) Ajoupa and bohio

3. Which of the following BEST describes the materials used to make these architectural structures?

(A) Wooden poles, mud and zinc
(B) Wooden poles, woven straw and palm leaves
(C) Wooden poles, stones and mortar
(D) Wooden poles, thatch and stones

4. What might account for the different shapes of the structures?

(A) To showcase social hierarchy
(B) To indicate artistic skills
(C) To represent cultural diversity
(D) To provide a functional advantage

---

5. All of the following Afro-Caribbean religions are correctly matched to the country they are practised EXCEPT

(A) Guyana --- Comfa
(B) Jamaica --- Myal
(C) Grenada --- Shango
(D) Haiti --- Santería

6. Which of the following does NOT illustrate the significance of Caribbean festivals in metropolitan countries?

   (A) They showcase Caribbean popular cultures, arts and music
   (B) They allow Caribbean cultures to gain international recognition
   (C) They showcase the solidary which exists in the Caribbean diaspora
   (D) They bring awareness to the level of poverty in the Caribbean

7. Which of the following artists have been dubbed the "first lady" of Nevisian art?

   (A) Edna Manley
   (B) Eva Wilkin
   (C) Goldie White
   (D) Heather Doram

8. A giclée is

   (A) a mural painting
   (B) a fine art print
   (C) an oil-based spray
   (D) a watercolour painting

9. Which of the following artists is credited for the design of the national dress of Antigua and Barbuda?

   (A) Edna Manley
   (B) Eva Wilkin
   (C) Goldie White
   (D) Heather Doram

10. Which of the following BEST describes intuitive art?

    (A) Expressionism
    (B) Surrealism
    (C) Abstractionism
    (D) Realism

11. Which of the following BEST describes a cenotaph?

    (A) A ceremonial tomb of a national hero or heroine
    (B) A type of tomb that is partially submerged in water
    (C) A monument built in honour of a person whose remains are elsewhere
    (D) A memorial structure that houses the reinterred remains of a person

12. Which of the following Caribbean cities is known for its colourful row houses with decorative wooden fretworks?

    (A) Havana, Cuba
    (B) San Juan, Puerto Rico
    (C) Willemstad, Curaçao
    (D) Port-au-Prince, Haiti

13. Which of the following European countries is most closely associated with the Baroque architectural style in the Caribbean?

    (A) Spain
    (B) Portugal
    (C) France
    (D) England

14. Which of the following is NOT a characteristic of Mayan architecture?

(A) Elaborate carvings and sculptures
(B) Use of corbeled arches
(C) Simple geometric shapes
(D) Hieroglyphic inscriptions

15. What is the name of the tool used to apply the wax or resist substance in batik?

(A) Stencil
(B) Brush
(C) Tjanting
(D) Stamp

16. What is the purpose of installation art?

(A) To be a visual representation of an idea or concept
(B) To sell something
(C) To create something visually appealing
(D) To be a form of entertainment

17. Which of the following is an example of installation art?

(A) A painting of a landscape
(B) A sculpture of a human figure
(C) A room filled with balloons
(D) A photograph of a flower

18. Which Jamaican artist created "Dead Treez" which was a garden-inspired installation referencing the victims of violent crime?

(A) Ebony G. Patterson
(B) Laura Facey
(C) Mallica Reynolds
(D) David Boxer

19. Who is the Trinidadian artist known for his use of recycled materials in his installation art?

(A) Peter Minshall
(B) Christopher Cozier
(C) Wendell McShine
(D) Richard Rawlins

20. Edna Manley is known as the "doyenne" of Jamaican art. In this context, this means that

(A) she was a prominent and respected figure in art
(B) she utilized various art techniques involving sculpture and pottery
(C) she is known solely for traditional art forms specific to Jamaica
(D) she utilized a method of art critique and analysis based on colour theory

Items 21 to 24 refer to the bronze National Windrush Monument based in London England and designed by the Jamaican artist, Basil Watson.

Source: https://commons.wikimedia.org/wiki/File:National_Windrush_ Monument,_2022-06-24.jpg (Retrieved 30th November 2024)

21. Which of the following BEST explain why bronze was used as the medium for the Windrush Monument?

(A) It can be painted with ease to protect it
(B) It is resistant to corrosion and weathering
(C) It disintegrates over time to create a natural patina
(D) It becomes softer with age, making repairs easier

22. What was the likely technique used by Watson to ensure the fine details of the Windrush Monument?

(A) Casting using a wax model
(B) Direct carving into the final materials
(C) Laser engraving
(D) Digital 3D printing

23. Who were the Windrush Generation in England?

(A) British-born individuals with Caribbean heritage
(B) European immigrants who travelled to the Caribbean after World War II
(C) African immigrants who arrived in England during the 1960s
(D) British soldiers who fought in the Falklands War

24. Which of the following was likely a strategy by Watson to achieve a lifelike representation of the figures in the Windrush Monument?

(A) Studying photographs and historical reference
(B) Using pre-made moulds from other sculptures
(C) Assembling pieces of fabric and metal
(D) Painting the monument to mimic realism

---

25. Fresco is a painting technique that involves applying pigments to a wet plaster surface. Which historical civilization is well-known for its extensive use of frescoes?

(A) Ancient Egypt
(B) Ancient Greece
(C) Mayan civilization
(D) Roman Empire

26. Self-taught artists are often referred to as

(A) outside artists
(B) installation artists
(C) unskilled artists
(D) traditional artists

27. What does the colour yellow represent in Kente cloth?

(A) Royalty
(B) Love
(C) Peace
(D) Fertility

28. What is the term for an artist who creates works that are outside of the traditional artistic conventions?

(A) Surreal
(B) Abstract
(C) Traditional
(D) Realistic

29. Which of the following organizations is responsible for collecting and exhibiting Jamaican art?

(A) Jamaica Guild of Artists
(B) Jamaica Cultural Development Commission
(C) National Gallery of Jamaica
(D) Jamaica Association of Vintage Artistes and Affiliates

30. Which of the following is a typical feature of Gothic architecture?

(A) Round arches
(B) Thick walls
(C) Minimal decoration
(D) Pointed arches

31. The largest Hindu sculpture in the Western Hemisphere is located in the Caribbean Island of

(A) Guyana
(B) Trinidad
(C) Belize
(D) Suriname

32. Which is a feature of an Ajoupa?

(A) Use of adobe bricks
(B) Elaborate carvings and decorations
(C) Circular or rectangular floor plans
(D) Tall and towering structures

33. Which of the following is a characteristic feature of Caribbean Impressionist paintings?

(A) Vibrant and bold colours
(B) Highly detailed and realistic depictions
(C) Depiction of urban scenes
(D) Use of chiaroscuro technique

34. Which element of art and design refers to the use of light and dark in a composition?

(A) Shape
(B) Colour
(C) Value
(D) Form

35. Which of the following is an art movement in the Caribbean?

(A) Garveyism
(B) Negritude
(C) Rastafari
(D) Harlem renaissance

36. Which of the following BEST depicts kinetic art?

(A) Art that reflects light
(B) Art that incorporates watercolours
(C) Art that depicts motion
(D) Art that is made using found objects

Items 37 to 40 refer to the image below which depicts a cannon at the Brimstone Hill Fortress National Park in the Caribbean.

Source: https://en.wikipedia.org/wiki/File:2016_02_FRD_Caribbean_Cruise_Brimstone_Hill_Fortress_Cannon_S0137034.jpg (retrieved 30th November 2024)

37. Which of the following BEST describes the cannon?

(A) Remnant
(B) Relic
(C) Artefact
(D) Feature

38. The Brimstone Hill Fortress National Park has been recognized as a World Heritage Site since 1999 due to its well-preserved military architecture. The fortress is located in

(A) Dominica
(B) St. Kitts and Nevis
(C) Barbados
(D) Antigua and Barbuda

39. Which of the following is the BEST strategy to prolong cannons such as that displayed in the photographic image?

(A) Display them outdoors in their original locations
(B) Store them in a humid environment to prevent corrosion
(C) Clean them regularly with abrasive materials to remove rust
(D) Implement a regular conservation and maintenance programme

40. Which of the following could account for why most cannon sites in the Caribbean are not recognized by UNESCO as World Heritage Sites?

(A) Lack of historical significance
(B) Insufficient preservation efforts
(C) Inadequate number of cannons
(D) Limited cultural impact

ANSWER KEY
PRACTICE EXAM 04

Item No.	Answer Key
1.	A
2.	A
3.	B
4.	A
5.	D
6.	D
7.	B
8.	B
9.	D
10.	A
11.	C
12.	C
13.	A
14.	C
15.	C
16.	A
17.	C
18.	A
19.	D
20.	A

Item No.	Answer Key
21.	B
22.	A
23.	A
24.	A
25.	D
26.	A
27.	A
28.	B
29.	C
30.	D
31.	B
32.	C
33.	A
34.	C
35.	B
36.	C
37.	C
38.	B
39.	D
40.	B

EXPLANATIONS FOR ANSWERS FOR PRACTICE EXAM 04

1. **(A)** The Taino, Ciboney and Garifuna's traditional architectural structures were typically thatched-roof huts or dwellings made from natural materials such as wood, thatch, and palm leaves. In contrast, the Maya were known for their impressive architectural achievements such as pyramids and palaces.

2. **(A)**The best names that describe the architectural structures as depicted in the image are bohio and caney. A bohio is a simple, traditional hut or dwelling made of natural materials like wood, thatch, and palm leaves. A caney, on the other hand, is a larger communal structure or longhouse where multiple families would live together. In the Taino communities, it was customary for caciques (leaders) to live in caneys, which also housed most of the ceremonial and religious objects. Bohio and caney were either rectangular or round.

3. **(B)** Wooden poles, woven straw, and palm leaves. Indigenous societies in the Caribbean and Central America commonly used wooden poles as the structural framework for their houses. These poles were often covered or thatched with woven straw and palm leaves to create the walls and roof of the structures. This combination of wooden poles, woven straw, and palm leaves provided a sturdy and natural construction suitable for the local climate and environment.

4. **(A)** The different shapes of the structures were often used to indicate social status and hierarchy within indigenous societies. Certain architectural designs and features were reserved for the dwellings of leaders or individuals of higher social standing, while others were used by the general population. The size, complexity, and adornments of the structures could convey the wealth, power, and importance of the occupants.

5. **(D)** Santería is not typically associated with Haiti. Santería is a religion that originated in Cuba and is primarily practised in Cuba and among Cuban diaspora communities. In Haiti, the predominant Afro-Caribbean religion is Vodou (also spelt Voodoo or Vodun). Vodou is a syncretic religion that combines elements of African traditional religions with Catholicism.

6. **(D)** Caribbean festivals in metropolitan countries primarily focus on celebrating and showcasing Caribbean popular cultures, arts, and music. They provide a platform for Caribbean communities to express their cultural identities and traditions, as well as promote cross-cultural exchange and understanding. These festivals also play a significant role in fostering a sense of solidarity among the Caribbean diaspora and promoting the recognition and appreciation of Caribbean cultures on an international level. Although these festivals are often used to bring awareness to various social issues from time to time, they are not specifically aimed at bringing awareness to the level of poverty in the Caribbean.

7. **(B)** Eva Wilkin (1898-1989) is known as the "first lady" of Nevisian art. She was born in Montserrat but moved to Nevis in 1925. She was a renowned artist who made significant contributions to the art scene in Nevis and the wider Caribbean. Her artwork often depicted the natural beauty and cultural heritage of Nevis, and she played a key role in promoting and preserving Nevisian art and culture.

8. **(B)** A giclée is a type of fine art print that is produced using high-quality inkjet printers. It is known for its exceptional colour accuracy and detail reproduction, often resembling the original artwork closely. Giclée prints are typically made on archival-quality paper or canvas and are popular among artists and collectors for their ability to capture the nuances of the original artwork.

9. **(D)** Heather Doram, an Antiguan artist and fashion designer, is credited with designing the national dress of Antigua and Barbuda. Her design which featured the madras plaid of red, gold and green was selected as the official national dress in 1992. The dress incorporates elements of traditional Antiguan and Barbudan culture and features vibrant colours, intricate patterns, and handcrafted details. Heather Doram's design has become an iconic symbol of the country's cultural heritage and is worn on special occasions and national celebrations. In recent years, Doram has been described as a "nationalist" artist given her many contributions to nation-building in her country.

10. **(A)** Intuitive art is often associated with expressionism, which emphasizes the artist's subjective and emotional response to the world. It is characterized by the artist's spontaneous and instinctual approach, focusing on the inner experience rather than an accurate representation of external reality. Intuitive art often involves bold brushwork, vibrant colours, and exaggerated forms to convey the artist's emotions and feelings. It allows for a free expression of ideas and encourages the exploration of the subconscious mind.

11. **(C)** A cenotaph is a memorial structure or monument that is built to honour a person or a group of people whose remains are not interred at that location. Cenotaphs are often erected as a symbolic tribute to individuals or events, particularly in cases where the actual burial site is located elsewhere. They serve as a place for remembrance and commemoration, even if the physical remains of the person being honoured are absent. Cenotaphs can be found in various forms, such as statues, pillars, or architectural structures, and they are commonly found in cemeteries, public spaces, or specific memorial sites.

12. **(C)** Willemstad, the capital city of Curaçao, is known for its colourful row houses with decorative wooden fretworks. The historic city centre of Willemstad, known as Punda and Otrobanda, features a distinctive architectural style influenced by Dutch colonial and Caribbean aesthetics. The row houses are characterized by their vibrant colours, often in shades of pastel, and ornate wooden trims and fretworks. The buildings reflect the unique cultural blend of Curaçao, showcasing the island's rich history and architectural heritage. The colourful and picturesque row houses of Willemstad have become an iconic symbol of the city and a popular attraction for visitors.

13. **(A)** The Baroque architectural style in the Caribbean is most closely associated with Spain. During the colonial period, many Caribbean islands were under Spanish control, including Cuba, Puerto Rico, and the Dominican Republic. Spanish colonial architecture greatly influenced the architectural landscape of these islands, and the Baroque style was particularly prominent. Baroque architecture is characterized by its ornate and extravagant features, including elaborate decoration, dramatic forms, and a sense of grandeur. In the Caribbean, Spanish colonial buildings often exhibit these characteristics, with intricate detailing, decorative facades, and a fusion of European and local influences.

14. **(C)** Mayan architecture is known for its elaborate carvings and sculptures, the use of corbeled arches, and hieroglyphic inscriptions. Mayan structures often exhibit intricate and detailed artwork, depicting various aspects of Mayan culture, history, and mythology. The architecture incorporates complex designs and decorative elements, showcasing the advanced artistic and architectural skills of the Mayan civilization. Simple geometric shapes are not a prominent characteristic of Mayan architecture, as the structures are typically more ornate and intricate in their design.

15. **(C)** A tjanting is a tool used in the art of batik to apply wax or a resistant substance onto fabric. It consists of a metal or wooden handle with a small spout or nozzle at the end. The artist uses the tjanting to control the flow of hot wax or resist and create intricate designs on the fabric. The size and shape of the nozzle can vary, allowing for different line thicknesses and patterns to be achieved in the batik process.

16. **(A)** Installation art is a form of contemporary art where the artist creates an entire environment or an immersive experience within a specific space. It goes beyond traditional art forms by utilizing various elements such as sculpture, multimedia, sound, video, and performance to transform the space and engage the viewer in a unique and thought-provoking way. The focus of installation art is often to convey a particular concept, theme, or message and to evoke emotional or intellectual responses from the audience. It can challenge traditional notions of art and blur the boundaries between art and the surrounding environment.

17. **(C)** Installation art typically involves creating an immersive environment or a specific spatial experience. It goes beyond traditional art forms such as paintings, sculptures, or photographs. In this case, a room filled with balloons would qualify as an installation art piece because it transforms the space and engages the viewer in a unique way. The balloons create a sensory and visually striking environment, altering the perception of the space and evoking a particular mood or response from the audience.

18. **(A)** Ebony G. Patterson, a Jamaican-born artist, is known for her thought-provoking installations that explore themes of identity, gender, and violence in the Caribbean context. "Dead Treez" is one of her notable installations that addresses the complex social issues surrounding death and mourning practices in Jamaica.

19. **(D)** Richard Rawlins is a Trinidadian artist known for his innovative use of recycled materials in his installation art. He often repurposes discarded objects and materials, transforming them into thought-provoking and visually striking installations. Rawlins' work explores themes of consumerism, waste, and environmental sustainability. His installations are known for their intricate craftsmanship and their ability to evoke contemplation and reflection in viewers.

20. **(A)** In the context of being referred to as the "doyenne" of Jamaican art, it means that Edna Manley was a highly esteemed and influential figure in the field of art, particularly in Jamaica. The term "doyenne" is used to describe a woman who is considered the most respected or prominent in a particular field or profession. Edna Manley played a significant role in the development and promotion of Jamaican art and is celebrated for her contributions as an artist, educator, and advocate for the arts. Her impact and influence have made her a revered figure in the art community, both in Jamaica and internationally.

21. **(B)** Bronze is a durable and versatile material commonly used in sculpture. Its resistance to corrosion and weathering makes it ideal for outdoor monuments, as it can withstand exposure to the elements without significant degradation. While bronze does develop a natural patina over time, this layer protects the underlying metal and adds an aesthetic quality to the sculpture, rather than signalling disintegration. Unlike materials that may degrade or require frequent maintenance, bronze ensures the longevity and preservation of the artwork.

22. (A) Watson likely used the technique of casting using a wax model. This technique is a traditional and effective method for creating intricate and detailed sculptures. This process involves creating a detailed model in wax, which is then encased in a mould. Once the mould is heated, the wax melts away, leaving a cavity that is filled with molten bronze. This technique allows artists to capture fine details, such as facial expressions and textures, which would be challenging to achieve through direct carving or other methods. Digital 3D printing and laser engraving are modern technologies but are less commonly used in traditional bronze sculpting.

23. (A) The Windrush Generation refers to the individuals who migrated from the Caribbean to England between 1948 and 1971. The name "Windrush" comes from the ship HMT Empire Windrush, which brought the first large group of Caribbean immigrants to the United Kingdom in 1948. The Windrush Generation primarily consisted of individuals from various Caribbean countries, including Jamaica, Trinidad and Tobago, Barbados, and other islands. They were invited to come to the United Kingdom to address labour shortages and help with post-war reconstruction efforts. The Windrush Generation and their descendants have made significant contributions to British society in various fields, including politics, arts and culture, sports, and education. They have played a vital role in shaping modern-day multicultural Britain. In recent years, the term "Windrush Generation" has gained prominence due to a scandal that arose in 2018. Many individuals from the Windrush Generation, who had lived in the United Kingdom for decades, were wrongly targeted by immigration policies and faced difficulties in proving their legal status. This led to an outcry and efforts to rectify the situation and provide justice for those affected.

24. (A) Artists often use historical references, including photographs, to accurately depict the appearance and essence of their subjects. This strategy allows them to capture realistic details such as clothing, facial expressions, and posture, ensuring the sculpture resonates with authenticity and historical accuracy. The use of pre-made moulds or fabric and metal would limit the individuality of the figures, and painting the monument would not be applicable to a bronze statue. Watson's use of references from the time period emphasizes the cultural and emotional impact of the Windrush Generation.

25. (D) Fresco painting was a popular and highly developed technique during the Roman Empire, particularly during the Roman Republic and the Roman Imperial period. Roman frescoes were commonly found in public buildings, villas, and tombs. They were used to decorate walls and ceilings, depicting various scenes such as mythology, historical events, landscapes, and portraits. Roman frescoes showcased the artistic skills and cultural expressions of the time. The process of creating a fresco involves applying pigments to freshly laid wet plaster, allowing the colours to seep into the plaster as it dries. This technique resulted in vibrant and long-lasting artworks. The Romans employed different types of fresco techniques, including the Buon fresco method, which involved painting on wet plaster, and the secco fresco method, which involved painting on dry plaster. While other ancient civilizations, such as the Ancient Egyptians and Ancient Greeks, also made use of frescoes in their artistic expressions, the Roman Empire is particularly renowned for the scale, variety, and quality of its fresco paintings.

26. **(A)** Self-taught artists are often referred to as "outside artists." This term is used to describe artists who have not received formal training or education in art institutions or academies. Instead, they develop their artistic skills and creative expression through their own experimentation, observation, and personal exploration. The term "outside artists" emphasizes the idea that these individuals exist outside the established art world and its conventional structures. They often work independently and create art on their own terms, outside of mainstream art movements and institutions. Self-taught artists may have unique perspectives, unconventional techniques, and a distinctive artistic voice that sets them apart from formally trained artists. The term "outside artists" is also sometimes used interchangeably with other terms like "folk artists," "naïve artists," or "outsider artists." These terms all refer to artists who operate outside of the traditional art establishment and may have unconventional backgrounds, including limited formal education or exposure to the art world.

27. **(A)** Kente cloth is known for its vibrant and intricate patterns, with each colour carrying symbolic meaning. The choice of colours in Kente cloth is significant and often reflects cultural, social, and historical contexts. Yellow is associated with wealth, power, and prestige in many African cultures, including those represented in Kente cloth. It is often used to symbolize the status and nobility of individuals, particularly those in positions of authority or leadership. Yellow is considered a regal colour and is sometimes reserved for special occasions or worn by royalty.

28. **(B)** Abstract art refers to artworks that do not attempt to represent an accurate depiction of visual reality. Instead, abstract artists use shapes, colours, forms, and gestural marks to achieve their artistic expression. They often emphasize subjective interpretation, emotional or expressive content, and non-representational or non-objective elements in their work. Abstract artists may explore concepts, sensations, or ideas through the use of form and colour, departing from the traditional techniques and styles associated with realistic or representational art.

29. **(C)** The National Gallery of Jamaica is the organization responsible for collecting and exhibiting Jamaican art. It is the oldest and largest public art museum in the English-speaking Caribbean. The gallery's mission is to collect, preserve, exhibit, and interpret Jamaican and other related art forms. It showcases a diverse range of artworks, including paintings, sculptures, ceramics, photographs, and mixed media installations, representing both historical and contemporary artists from Jamaica and the wider Caribbean region. The other options are also important organizations in the Jamaican arts and culture scene, but they do not specifically focus on collecting and exhibiting Jamaican art to the same extent as the National Gallery of Jamaica.

30. **(D)** Pointed arches are one of the distinctive features of Gothic architecture. Unlike the rounded arches commonly found in Romanesque architecture, Gothic architecture introduced the use of pointed arches. These arches are formed by two curved lines that meet at the apex, creating a pointed shape. Pointed arches were not only aesthetically pleasing but also had structural advantages, allowing for taller and more spacious buildings with larger windows. This architectural feature is characteristic of Gothic cathedrals and other structures of the Gothic period.

31. (B) The largest Hindu sculpture in the Western Hemisphere is located in the Caribbean Island of Trinidad. The sculpture is located in Carapichaima, Trinidad. It is a massive 85-foot-tall statue of Lord Hanuman, a deity in Hinduism. Lord Hanuman is a Hindu god regarded as the most revered disciple of Lord Rama who exhibited great strength and bravery. The statue is the largest Hanuman murti outside of India and is a prominent landmark and a significant religious site for the Hindu community in Trinidad and Tobago.

32. (C) An ajoupa is a traditional Caribbean indigenous dwelling, commonly found in the Caribbean islands. It is a small, simple structure typically made of natural materials such as wood, thatch, bamboo and woven palm leaves. Ajoupas are known for their practical and functional design, with circular or rectangular floor plans that provide shelter and protection from the elements. They are often open-sided or have minimal walls to allow for ventilation in the warm Caribbean climate.

33. (A) Caribbean Impressionist paintings often feature vivid and vibrant colours that capture the vibrant nature and tropical landscapes of the Caribbean region. The artists use bold and expressive brushstrokes to depict the play of light and colour in their subjects, conveying a sense of immediacy and capturing the atmospheric effects of the Caribbean environment. The use of bright and lively colours is a distinguishing feature of Caribbean Impressionist paintings, reflecting the region's vibrant culture and natural surroundings.

34. (C) Value in art refers to the range of lightness and darkness within an artwork. It is determined by the amount of light that is reflected or absorbed by different areas of a composition. Value is often represented through a grayscale, ranging from white to black, with various shades of grey in between. By manipulating the values in a composition, artists can create a sense of depth, volume, and contrast. It helps to define the forms and shapes within the artwork, and it contributes to the overall mood and atmosphere.

35. (B) Negritude was a literary and cultural movement that emerged in the 1930s among French-speaking black intellectuals from the Caribbean and Africa. It aimed to celebrate and affirm black identity, culture, and heritage in response to colonialism and racial discrimination. Negritude encompassed various art forms, including poetry, literature, visual arts, and music, and it sought to promote a positive and empowering image of blackness. The movement emphasized the beauty, history, and contributions of black people and played a significant role in the development of Caribbean and African cultural movements.

36. (C) Kinetic art is a form of art that incorporates movement as a key element. It typically includes artworks that physically move, create an illusion of movement, or involve viewer participation. The artwork may involve mechanical or technological components, use natural forces like wind or water, or rely on optical illusions to create the impression of motion. Kinetic art explores the dynamic and changing aspects of the artwork, engaging the viewer in a unique and interactive experience.

37. **(C)** The best term to describe the cannon as depicted in the image is artefact. Artefacts are objects that are made or modified by humans and have cultural or historical significance. The cannon in the image is a man-made object that was used for military purposes. They have historical and cultural value as they are remnants of the past and are associated with the history of Fort Charles in Jamaica. While the terms "remnant" (A) and "relic" (B) can also be used to describe the cannon, the term "artefact" specifically emphasizes its cultural and historical significance. The term "feature" (D) does not accurately describe the cannon as it is a generic term.

38. **(B)** The Brimstone Hill Fortress National Park is located in St. Kitts and Nevis and has been recognized as a World Heritage Site since 1999 for its well-preserved military architecture. It is a significant historical and cultural site that showcases the military architecture of the colonial era. The fortress was constructed by the British starting in the late 17th Century and played a crucial role in defending the island and its valuable sugar plantations against rival European powers. The well-preserved fortifications, including the walls, bastions, barracks, and other structures, exemplify the military engineering and design of the time. The site offers a glimpse into the strategic importance of St. Kitts during the colonial period and provides insights into the history and conflicts in the Caribbean region.

39. **(D)** The best strategy to prolong the cannons such as that displayed in the photographic image is by implementing a regular conservation and maintenance programme. Cannons, being historical artefacts made of metal, require proper care and preservation to prevent deterioration and ensure their longevity. Implementing a regular conservation and maintenance programme is essential for their preservation. The other options might not be ideal. Displaying the cannons outdoors in their original locations (A) may expose them to harsh weather conditions and accelerate their deterioration. Storing them in a humid environment (B) can promote corrosion and damage. Cleaning the cannons with abrasive materials (C) can cause irreparable damage to the metal surfaces.

40. **(B)** UNESCO World Heritage Sites are selected based on their outstanding universal value, which includes criteria such as their historical, cultural, or natural significance. Cannon sites in the Caribbean can indeed have historical and cultural significance, given their association with colonialism, military history, and the region's heritage. However, many of these sites may lack proper preservation efforts, which can prevent them from meeting the criteria for UNESCO recognition. Preservation efforts are crucial for maintaining the integrity and authenticity of sites. Insufficient preservation efforts may lead to the deterioration and loss of the cannons and associated structures over time. This can impact the overall value and potential for recognition as a World Heritage Site. While options (A), (C), and (D) can contribute to a site's eligibility for UNESCO recognition, they are not the primary reasons why most cannon sites in the Caribbean are not recognized. Historical significance, the number of cannons, and cultural impact can vary across different sites, and they may still be considered for recognition if proper preservation efforts are in place.

CAPE®

ART AND DESIGN

PRACTISE TEST 05

Paper 01

1 hour 30 minutes

READ THE FOLLOWING INSTRUCTIONS CAREFULLY.

1. This Practice Test consists of 40 items.

2. You will have 1 hour 30 minutes to answer them.

3. Each item in this Practice Test has four suggested answers lettered (A), (B), (C) and (D). Read each item and decide on the best choice. Look at the sample item below.

Sample Item:

Which Cuban artist was known for his depiction of Afro-Cuban religious iconography in his art?

(A) José Bedia
(B) Wifredo Lam
(C) Roberto Fabelo
(D) Carlos Garaicoa

Sample Answer:

The best answer to this item is "Wifredo Lam" and so (B) is shaded.

4. When you are told to begin, turn the page and work as quickly and as carefully as you can. If you cannot answer an item, go on to the next one and return to this item later.

RLF Publications.
"... redefining publishing..."

1. What was the purpose of petroglyphs?

(A) To provide entertainment for people
(B) To record historical events and stories
(C) To serve as a form of currency
(D) To create abstract designs

2. All of the following were techniques used to create pottery in Indigenous Caribbean society EXCEPT

(A) Coiling
(B) Burnishing
(C) Firing
(D) Glazing

3. Which of the following is NOT a common element in Afro-Cuban religious art?

(A) Use of bright colours
(B) Depictions of deities
(C) Use of geometric shapes
(D) Depictions of animals

4. Who is known as the father of Caribbean Impressionism?

(A) John Dunkley
(B) Carlisle Chang
(C) Harold Simmons
(D) Albert Huie

5. In which Caribbean country is the "Jab Jab" body painting tradition practised which involves the application of black substance such as oil, charcoal or body paint?

(A) Grenada
(B) Jamaica
(C) Bahamas
(D) Barbados

6. What is the traditional significance of henna among Hindus in the Caribbean?

(A) It is used as a decorative art form for special occasions
(B) It is believed to ward off evil spirits and bring good luck
(C) It is used for medicinal purposes
(D) It is a symbol of social status and wealth

7. Kinetic art is generally based on

(A) surrealism
(B) fauvism
(C) cubism
(D) impressionism

8. The Trinidad artist Shawn Peters is known for artwork that depicts Caribbean cubism. Which of the following BEST describes Caribbean cubism?

(A) A realistic depiction of Caribbean landscapes and folklore
(B) An abstract art style that deconstructs forms into geometric shapes influenced by African, European, and Caribbean aesthetics
(C) A hyper-realistic art form focusing on the daily lives of Caribbean people
(D) A minimalist approach emphasizing simplicity and monochromatic colour schemes

Items 9 and 11 below relate to the image of a group of women wearing the National dress of Jamaica.

Photographer unknown.
Source: https://www.workandjam.com/news/13-things-to-know-about-the-jamaican-national-costume.htm (retrieved 30th November 2024)

9. Which of the following BEST describes the dress being worn by the women?

(A) A Madras dress
(B) A Quadrille dress
(C) A Kwadril dress
(D) An Adinkra dress

10. Other than Jamaica, which other Caribbean country might have a similar dress as its national dress?

(A) Barbados, and Trinidad and Tobago
(B) Dominica and Haiti
(C) Antigua and Barbuda, and St. Lucia
(D) Guyana and Grenada

11. As depicted by the image, what art forms are often associated with the national dresses of the various Caribbean countries?

(A) Painting and photography
(B) Street theatre and dancing
(C) Parading and masquerades
(D) Storytelling and performance art

12. Which was NOT a utilitarian purpose of pottery in indigenous societies?

(A) To make ceremonial items and masks
(B) To craft hunting tools
(C) To create musical instruments
(D) To form cooking vessels

13. Which of the following materials is the least likely to be used in installation art in the Caribbean?

(A) Recycled cardboard
(B) Glass and steel
(C) Plants and stones
(D) Old newspaper

14. What is the technique used to create masks using metal?

(A) Welding
(B) Casting
(C) Carving
(D) Moulding

15. What is the primary animal source used to make red dye in traditional Caribbean culture?

(A) Beetles
(B) Crustaceans
(C) Insects
(D) Cochineal bugs

16. Which of the following is a characteristic of African art?

(A) Use of bright colours
(B) Realistic portrayal of the human form
(C) Symmetrical design
(D) Depiction of historical events

17. Which of the following features was often included in the design of plantation homes in the Caribbean up to the 1800s for ventilation and cooling?

(A) Cellar and chimneys
(B) Asphalt shingles
(C) Louvred windows
(D) Thatched roofs

18. Which of the following is the most prominent characteristic of Caribbean genre paintings?

(A) Use of bright, bold colours
(B) Depiction of mythical creatures
(C) Emphasis on geometric shapes
(D) Focus on religious iconography

19. Which of the following is NOT a requirement for copyright protection of a work of art?

(A) The artwork must be original
(B) The artwork must be tangible
(C) The artwork must be published
(D) The artwork must be created by a human being

20. What was a "maraca" in indigenous Caribbean societies?

(A) A stone weapon
(B) A musical instrument
(C) A straw hut
(D) A sling made of fabric

Items 21 to 23 refer to the image below which reflects a typical dwelling structure found in slave communities in the British West Indies in the early 19th Century.

Image is in the public domain and used pursuant to the Creative Commons License via Wikimedia. "Wood Plank House, St. Vincent, West Indies, ca. 1898" in Robert T. Hill, Cuna and Porto Rico (New York, 1898).

21. Other than thatched roofs, which of the following was a feature of the dwelling structure depicted in the image?

(A) Lath and plaster
(B) Wattle and daub
(C) Stucco and blocks
(D) Bricks and mortar

22. Which of the following BEST describes the dwelling structure in the image?

(A) Vernacular house
(B) Shanks house
(C) Adobe house
(D) Palafito house

23. Which of the following was NOT a feature of the dwelling structure of enslaved people in the British West Indies in the early 19th Century?

(A) Limited ventilation
(B) Small and cramped spaces
(C) Sufficient privacy
(D) Minimal amenities

24. What is the MAIN purpose of art criticism?

(A) To determine the market value of an artwork
(B) To analyse and interpret the meaning of an artwork
(C) To judge an artwork based on personal taste
(D) To promote the artist or art movement

25. What was the subject matter of Agostino Brunias' paintings in the Caribbean?

(A) Landscapes
(B) Portraits of colonial officials
(C) Scenes of plantation life
(D) Religious imagery

26. Which was NOT a common theme in the paintings of itinerant artists in the Caribbean in the pre-emancipation period?

(A) Landscapes and seascapes
(B) Portraits of plantation owners
(C) Scenes of enslaved people working
(D) Hindu temples and customs

27. What is the MAIN characteristic of Optical Art?

(A) Bold colours and gestural brushstrokes
(B) Flat planes of colour and hard edges
(C) Distorted shapes and dreamlike scenes
(D) Naturalistic depictions of everyday life

Items 28 to 30 refer to the image below which reflects Kalinago stone heads in a Caribbean territory.

Image © Uncommon Caribbean
Source: https://www.uncommoncaribbean.com (retrieved 30th November 2024)

28. Which of the following Caribbean territories is associated with the Kalinago stone heads?

(A) Guyana
(B) Barbados
(C) Dominica
(D) Grenada

29. What might have been the purpose of the Kalinago stone heads?

(A) To represent deities or leaders
(B) To represent the ancestral burial markers
(C) To symbolize military strength and power
(D) To demonstrate artistic capabilities

30. Which of the following BEST describes the significance of the Kalinago stone heads?

(A) They serve as landmarks for tourist attractions
(B) They provide insights into the artistic skills of the Kalinago people
(C) They are used in traditional ceremonies and rituals by the Kalinago community
(D) They highlight the utilization of Indigenous materials

---

31. Which of the following materials was commonly used for the construction of colonial churches and administrative buildings in the Caribbean?

(A) Brick
(B) Concrete
(C) Timber
(D) Steel

32. What was the primary purpose of art in indigenous societies in the pre-Columbian period?

(A) To celebrate the beauty of nature and landscapes
(B) To communicate religious and mythological beliefs
(C) To depict everyday life and social interactions
(D) To showcase the wealth and power of the ruling elite

33. Which is the MOST common technique used in Caribbean quilting?

(A) Weaving
(B) Embroidery
(C) Applique
(D) Macrame

34. Which of the following artists would most likely engage in intuitive painting?

(A) Jessica who has no formal art training and wishes to explore aspects of her inner self
(B) John who studied art for several years wants to appeal to a wide audience
(C) Sam who is self-taught but hopes to develop a commercially viable style of art
(D) Mary has years of training but has not yet received critical acclaim for her realistic paintings

35. Which of the following metropolitan cities is NOT known for hosting annual Caribbean festivals?

(A) Toronto
(B) New York
(C) London
(D) Chicago

36. Which of the following is true of lithography?

(A) It produces prints with vibrant and saturated colours
(B) It allows for the creation of textured and three-dimensional prints
(C) It enables the artist to create prints with a wide range of tonal values
(D) It produces prints with a distinct and grainy texture

Items 37 to 40 refer to the image below which depicts the painting entitled "Damballah La Flambeau" by the Haitian artist Hector Hyppolite. The painting captures a serpent-like spirit (loa) with a human face.

Image is in the public domain and is used pursuant Wikimedia Commons Licence. https://commons.wikimedia.org/wiki/File:Damballah_La_Flambeau.jpg (retrieved 30th November 2024)

37. Which of the following BEST captures the themes in Hyppolite's artwork as exemplified by the image?

(A) The hyper-realistic depictions of natural landscapes and serene human expressions
(B) The abstraction of shapes to depict movement and light in religious themes
(C) The fusion of human, mythological and symbolic elements
(D) The fragmentation of geometric shapes and objects to evoke religious imagery

38. Which of the following influences is MOST prominent in the artwork?

(A) Cubism
(B) Realism
(C) Modernism
(D) Surrealism

39. Which of the following Afro-Caribbean religions might have influenced Hyppolite's artwork?

(A) Vodun
(B) Rastafari
(C) Santeria
(D) Revivalism

40. The bottom of the artwork features various flowers. What is the likely symbolism of flowers in Hyppolite's artwork?

(A) Decorative elements with no deeper significance
(B) Symbols of colonial oppression and resistance
(C) Abstract representations of natural beauty
(D) Attributes of deities, representing their qualities or powers

END OF TEST

ANSWER KEY FOR PRACTICE TEST 05

Item No.	Answer Key
1.	B
2.	D
3.	C
4.	D
5.	A
6.	A
7.	A
8.	B
9.	B
10.	B
11.	D
12.	B
13.	B
14.	B
15.	D
16.	C
17.	C
18.	A
19.	C
20.	B

Item No.	Answer Key
21.	B
22.	A
23.	C
24.	B
25.	C
26.	D
27.	B
28.	C
29.	A
30.	B
31.	A
32.	B
33.	C
34.	A
35.	D
36.	C
37.	C
38.	D
39.	A
40.	D

EXPLANATIONS FOR ANSWERS FOR PRACTICE TEST 05

1. **(B)** The purpose of petroglyphs, ancient rock carvings or engravings, was primarily to record historical events and stories. Petroglyphs can be found in various parts of the world and were often created by indigenous peoples or ancient civilizations. They served as a form of communication and expression, documenting important aspects of their culture, including historical events, mythologies, spiritual beliefs, hunting practices, and daily life. In modern times, these rock art depictions provide valuable insights into the past, allowing us to study and understand the cultures that created them.

2. **(D)** In Indigenous Caribbean societies, the technique of glazing was not typically used to create pottery. Glazing is a process of applying a glass-like coating to the surface of pottery, which enhances its appearance and provides a protective layer. Glazing originated in the 4th millennium BC by the Ancient Egyptians. However, the Indigenous people in the Caribbean likely employed such techniques as coiling, burnishing, and firing to make their pottery. Coiling (A) is a method of constructing pottery by rolling or coiling long strands of clay and layering them on top of each other to form the desired shape. Burnishing (B) involves smoothing the surface of the pottery by rubbing it with a hard object like a stone or shell, giving it a polished appearance. Firing (D) refers to the process of baking the pottery in a kiln or open fire to harden it and make it durable. These techniques were commonly used in indigenous Caribbean societies to create their pottery.

3. **(C)** Afro-Cuban religious art often incorporates vibrant and bold colours (A), symbolizing the energetic and spiritual nature of the religion. They also depict deities, such as Orishas (divine beings in the Afro-Cuban religion) (B). These deities are often depicted in various forms, representing their different characteristics and attributes. Additionally, animals (D) are commonly seen in Afro-Cuban religious art as they hold symbolic significance and are associated with specific deities or spiritual entities. However, the use of geometric shapes (C) is not typically seen in Afro-Cuban religious art. The focus tends to be more on representing the spiritual and mythical aspects of the religion through the use of colour, deity depictions, and animal symbolism.

4. **(D)** Albert Huie (1920-2010) is known as the father of Caribbean Impressionism. He was a Jamaican painter who played a significant role in the development and popularization of the Impressionist style in the Caribbean region. Huie's artwork often depicted scenes from daily life in Jamaica, capturing the vibrant colours, light, and atmosphere of the Caribbean with loose brushwork and a focus on capturing the impression of a moment.

5. **(A)** The "Jab Jab" body painting tradition is practised in Grenada. The term "Jab Jab" refers to a traditional masquerade character in Grenadian Carnival celebrations. Participants in the Jab Jab tradition cover their bodies with black substances, often including molasses, oil, or even tar. This practice has historical and cultural significance, representing resistance, endurance, and the celebration of African

heritage in Grenada. The Jab Jab tradition is an integral part of Grenada's Carnival festivities and is known for its vibrant and energetic displays.

6. **(A)** Henna holds traditional significance as a decorative art form for special occasions. Henna, also known as mehndi, is a natural dye derived from the henna plant. It is used to create intricate and temporary designs on the skin, typically on the hands and feet, using a cone-shaped applicator. Hindus in the Caribbean often use henna during religious and cultural celebrations, such as weddings, festivals, and religious ceremonies. The application of henna is considered a form of adornment and beautification, enhancing the appearance of individuals and symbolizing joy and celebration. The designs can be elaborate and artistic, showcasing cultural motifs and symbols.

7. **(A)** Surrealism is an art movement that emerged in the early 20th Century, characterized by its exploration of the subconscious mind, dreams, and irrational elements. Surrealist artists sought to depict and evoke a sense of the fantastical, the unexpected, and the irrational in their works. Kinetic art, with its emphasis on movement and often unconventional or unexpected elements, shares a connection with the principles of Surrealism. Surrealist artists sought to challenge traditional notions of art and reality, often incorporating elements of surprise, transformation, and motion in their creations. The use of movement in kinetic art can evoke a sense of the surreal, as objects or elements seem to come alive or defy gravity, creating an otherworldly or dreamlike experience for the viewer.

8. **(B)** Caribbean Cubism is an art form that adapts the foundational principles of traditional European Cubism, which emphasizes the breaking down of objects into geometric forms to depict multiple perspectives simultaneously. However, it diverges significantly from its European roots by incorporating the rich cultural heritage of the Caribbean. Artists like Shawn Peters reinterpret the Caribbean's vibrant landscapes, people, and culture by deconstructing them into geometric forms. This allows viewers to experience the artwork as a layered and multifaceted representation of the Caribbean spirit. The other options do not capture the essence of cubism. Options (A) and (C) focus on realism which does not align with cubism's abstract nature. Option (D) refers to minimalism, characterized by simplicity and lack of colour, which contrasts the vibrant and complex visual language of Caribbean Cubism.

9. **(B)** The national dress of Jamaica is known as a Quadrille dress. The Quadrille dress is a traditional Jamaican attire that originated from the European quadrille dance, which was popular in the 18th and 19th centuries. It is characterized by its colourful and vibrant design, often featuring bold patterns and multiple layers. The dress typically consists of a full, ankle-length skirt with ruffled or pleated details, a fitted bodice, and puffed sleeves. It is commonly worn during cultural events, festivals, and special occasions in Jamaica, representing the country's rich cultural heritage and traditions.

10. (B) Dominica and Haiti are two other Caribbean countries that have similar dresses as the national dress of Jamaica and feature aspects of the Quadrille dress, although they are named differently. In Dominica, the quadrille dress is called the wob dwiyet. It is a traditional dress characterized by a long, flowing gown made from brightly coloured fabric. The dress is often accompanied by headscarves, aprons, and other accessories. In Haiti, the quadrille dress is known as the Karabela dress. It is a traditional dress that reflects the cultural heritage of the Haitian people. The dress typically features vibrant colours, intricate embroidery, and decorative elements. It is often worn on special occasions and cultural events in Haiti. Option (C) is partially correct. The quadrille dress is also worn in St. Lucia and is called the kwadril dress. However, it is not worn in Antigua and Barbuda.

11. (D) Based on the image of the women, and within the context of the national dresses of the various Caribbean countries, the art form often associated with these dresses is storytelling and performance art. The image suggests a theatrical and performative aspect associated with the national dresses. These dresses are often worn during cultural events, festivals, and celebrations where storytelling and performance art play a significant role. Through music, dance, and theatrical presentations, performers convey narratives, legends, and cultural stories that are deeply rooted in Caribbean traditions and history. The national dresses serve as visual representations of these narratives, adding to the overall artistic and performative experience.

12. (B) Pottery in indigenous societies had utilitarian purposes such as creating cooking vessels, storage containers, domestic utensils, ceremonial items, masks and musical instruments. While the art of pottery allowed for the creation of many useful items in indigenous societies, it was not typically used for crafting hunting tools. Hunting tools, such as spears, bows and arrows, traps, and other implements, were usually made from materials such as wood, bone, stone, or metal, depending on the resources available in the specific indigenous culture.

13. (B) Among the options provided, glass and steel are the least likely materials to be used in installation art in the Caribbean. While installation art can encompass a wide range of materials, the availability and use of glass and steel might be limited in the Caribbean due to factors such as cost, accessibility, and cultural context. Indeed, glass and steel may be less commonly used due to the higher cost and limited availability of these materials, especially in remote or economically disadvantaged regions. Additionally, the use of glass and steel might be influenced by the cultural context and the preference for more organic or locally sourced materials in Caribbean installation art. Recycled cardboard, plants, stones, and old newspapers are materials that are commonly found and used in installation art in the Caribbean. Recycling and repurposing materials, including cardboard and newspaper, align with sustainability practices and the utilization of available resources. Plants and stones are often incorporated to establish a connection with nature and the local environment.

14. **(B)** Metal casting involves pouring molten metal into a mould and allowing it to cool and solidify, resulting in the desired shape. For mask-making, a mould is created with the desired mask design, and molten metal, such as bronze or aluminium, is poured into the mould. Once the metal solidifies, the mould is removed, leaving behind a metal mask with the intricacies and details captured in the casting process. Metal casting is a common technique used in various forms of metal art, including mask-making. It allows for the creation of highly detailed and intricate metal masks, and it offers flexibility in terms of the metal used and the variety of designs that can be achieved.

15. **(D)** In traditional Caribbean culture, the primary animal source used to make red dye is cochineal bugs. Cochineal bugs are small insects that are native to Central and South America. The female cochineal bugs are rich in carminic acid, a natural pigment that produces a vibrant red colour. To obtain the red dye, the bugs are harvested from their host plants, dried, and then crushed to extract the carminic acid. This dye has been used for centuries in various cultural practices, including textile dyeing, artwork, and traditional crafts in the Caribbean and other parts of the world.

16. **(C)** Symmetry is a prevalent characteristic in many forms of African art. It can be observed in various art forms, including masks, sculptures, textiles, and architectural elements. Symmetry in African art often involves the balanced arrangement of elements, patterns, and forms on either side of a central axis. This symmetrical approach reflects a sense of harmony, balance, and order in the artwork. While African art can incorporate a wide range of colours (A), including bright colours, it is not exclusively defined by the use of bright colours. African art also embraces a wide spectrum of colour palettes, including earth tones, muted hues, and natural pigments. Similarly, African art often employs stylized and abstract representations of the human form rather than a strict emphasis on realistic portrayal (B). This allows for a range of expressive and symbolic interpretations. Finally, while African art can sometimes depict historical events (D), it is not a defining characteristic of the entire corpus of African art. Historical events are often represented through oral traditions, storytelling, and performance art in African cultures, rather than solely through visual art forms.

17. **(C)** Louvred windows were often included in the design of plantation homes in the Caribbean up to the 1800s for ventilation and cooling. Louvred windows have adjustable slats or blades that can be opened or closed to control the flow of air. By adjusting the angle of the slats, plantation homeowners could regulate the amount of airflow entering the house, allowing for better ventilation and natural cooling. This was particularly important in the Caribbean's warm and tropical climate, where maintaining a comfortable indoor temperature was essential. While other features, such as cellars and chimneys (A), might have been present in some plantation homes, they were not primarily included for ventilation and cooling purposes. Asphalt shingles (B) were not commonly used in the design of plantation homes during that time period. Thatched roofs (D), while providing insulation and some airflow, were not typically used in larger plantation homes and were more common in traditional vernacular architecture in rural areas.

18. (A) A characteristic of Caribbean genre painting is the use of bright, bold colours. Caribbean genre painting often reflects the vibrant and diverse cultural heritage of the region, and artists frequently employ a vivid colour palette to depict scenes of everyday life, cultural traditions, and landscapes. These colours contribute to the energetic and lively atmosphere often found in Caribbean genre paintings. While mythical creatures (A) and religious iconography (D) may appear in some Caribbean artwork, they are not defining characteristics of Caribbean genre painting. Emphasis on geometric shapes (C) is not a prevalent feature specific to Caribbean genre painting. Instead, Caribbean genre painting tends to focus on capturing the everyday experiences, social interactions, and cultural practices of the Caribbean people, often incorporating elements of realism and narrative storytelling.

19. (C) Publishing an artwork is not a requirement for copyright protection. Copyright protection automatically applies to an original work of art as soon as it is created and fixed in a tangible form. For a work of art to be eligible for copyright protection, it must meet the requirements at options (A), (B) and (D). The work must be independently created by the author and possess some level of creativity. It should not be a copy of someone else's work. Additionally, the work must be fixed in a tangible medium, such as a painting on canvas, a sculpture, or a digital file. Ideas or concepts alone are not protected by copyright. Moreover, copyright protection generally applies to works created by human beings and does not extend to works created by animals or natural forces. Publication, which refers to making the artwork available to the public, is not a requirement for copyright protection. However, copyright registration or placing a copyright notice on the artwork can provide additional legal benefits and protections.

20. (B) In indigenous Caribbean societies, a "maraca" refers to a musical instrument. Maracas are percussion instruments typically made from gourds or calabash fruits. They consist of hollowed-out gourds filled with seeds, beans, or other small objects. When shaken, the seeds inside the gourd produce rhythmic sounds. Maracas were commonly used in traditional music and dances of the indigenous Caribbean peoples. They played a significant role in cultural and ceremonial activities, adding rhythm and musical accompaniment to songs and dances. Today, maracas are still widely used in various musical genres and are often associated with Caribbean and Latin American music.

21. (B) Other than thatched roofs, a feature commonly found in slave quarters in the early 19th Century was wattle and daub construction. Wattle and daub is a traditional building technique that involves weaving thin branches or wooden strips (wattle) together and then coating them with a mixture of mud, clay, and straw (daub). This technique was used to create walls and partitions in many historical structures, including slave quarters. Wattle and daub provided insulation and some structural stability while being relatively inexpensive and readily available. Lath and plaster (A), stucco and blocks (C), and bricks and mortar (D) were less common in slave quarters during that time period. Lath and plaster involve applying a layer of plaster onto a framework of wooden laths, which was a more complex and expensive construction method. Stucco and blocks refer to using a stucco coating over concrete or masonry blocks. Bricks and mortar were materials and techniques typically associated with more substantial or formal constructions rather than the modest dwellings of slave quarters.

22. **(A)** The structure depicted in the image can be described as a vernacular house. Vernacular architecture refers to the traditional, indigenous, or local style of building that is characteristic of a specific region, culture, or community. Vernacular houses are typically constructed using locally available materials and adapted to suit the climate, environment, and cultural needs of the community. In the context of the image, the house represents a typical structure found in slave communities in the British West Indies in the early 19th Century. It exhibits elements of vernacular architecture, such as the use of natural materials and construction techniques suitable for the local conditions. Vernacular houses often reflect the cultural and historical context of the region and are designed to meet the practical needs of the community.

23. **(C)** Enslaved people often lived in overcrowded and cramped spaces, with limited access to personal privacy. The living quarters provided to enslaved individuals were often small and confined, with multiple people forced to share limited space. These living conditions did not afford much privacy for individuals or families. On the other hand, options (A), (B) and (D) are true about the living conditions of enslaved people. Enslaved people often had limited ventilation (A) in their living spaces, as adequate airflow and ventilation were not prioritized in the construction of slave quarters. The spaces were often poorly ventilated, leading to uncomfortable and unhealthy living conditions. Additionally, enslaved individuals were provided with minimal amenities (D), with basic necessities often lacking or inadequate.

24. **(B)** The main purpose of art criticism is to analyse and interpret the meaning, aesthetic qualities, and cultural significance of an artwork. Art critics engage with artworks to provide thoughtful analysis and evaluation based on their knowledge and expertise in the field of art. They examine the formal elements, technique, style, historical context, and thematic content of the artwork to develop interpretations and insights. Art criticism goes beyond personal taste or subjective judgment. It aims to offer a deeper understanding of the artwork, its context, and the intentions of the artist. Art critics may explore the symbolism, social commentary, artistic techniques, and cultural references present in the artwork. They may also consider the historical, political, and cultural context in which the artwork was created, providing valuable insights into its meaning and significance.

25. **(C)** The subject matter of Agostino Brunias' paintings in the Caribbean primarily focused on scenes of plantation life. Brunias was an Italian-born artist who lived and worked in the Caribbean during the late 18th Century. His paintings often depicted scenes of everyday life in the colonial Caribbean, particularly in the islands of Dominica, Antigua, and St. Vincent. Brunias' works captured the diverse activities and social dynamics of plantation life, showcasing scenes of enslaved labourers, plantation owners, and the local population. He depicted various aspects of plantation culture, including agricultural work, domestic scenes, marketplaces, festivals, and social gatherings. His paintings often portrayed the relationships and power dynamics between the different social groups present in the Caribbean at that time. Brunias' paintings provide important visual documentation of the Caribbean during the colonial era and offer insights into the social and cultural dynamics of plantation society. While he may have also depicted landscapes and portraits on occasion, his notable and distinctive body of work primarily revolved around scenes of plantation life.

26. **(D)** During the pre-emancipation period in the Caribbean, itinerant artists, also known as "limners," travelled around the islands creating paintings for the local population. Their works often depicted various aspects of Caribbean life and society. While landscapes and seascapes (A), portraits of plantation owners (B), and scenes of enslaved people working (C) were common themes in their paintings, Hindu temples and customs were not typically portrayed. The majority of itinerant artists in the Caribbean during that period were focused on capturing scenes and subjects related to colonial society, plantations, and the lives of the European elite and enslaved individuals. East Indians, along with their culture and religion, came to the Caribbean in the post-emancipation period.

27. **(B)** The main characteristic of Optical Art, also known as Op Art, is the use of flat planes of colour and hard edges to create optical illusions and visual effects. Op Art emerged in the 1960s and was influenced by geometric abstraction and the study of perceptual psychology. Op Art artists sought to create artworks that appeared to be in motion or to produce visual vibrations through the manipulation of geometric forms and patterns. They employed precise and repetitive arrangements of lines, shapes, and colours to create the illusion of movement, depth, or shifting perspectives. The focus on flatness, hard edges, and the precise arrangement of visual elements distinguishes Op Art from other artistic styles. The artworks often create optical illusions that challenge the viewer's perception and create a sense of visual dynamism and optical effects. While Op Art may incorporate bold colours, it is the specific use of flat planes and hard edges to create optical illusions that is its defining characteristic.

28. **(C)** The Kalinago stone heads depicted in the image are associated with the Caribbean territory of Dominica. The Kalinago people, also known as the Caribs, were one of the indigenous groups inhabiting the Caribbean islands before the arrival of Europeans. Dominica has a rich history and cultural heritage linked to the Kalinago people. The stone heads, known as "Kalinago stone carvings" or "Kalinago stone heads," are a significant archaeological and cultural feature found on the island. These stone carvings are believed to have been created by the Kalinago people and are considered important symbols of their heritage.

29. **(A)** The likely purpose of the Kalinago stone heads was to represent deities or leaders within the Kalinago culture. These stone carvings were likely created to depict important figures of religious or political significance. The Kalinago people had a rich spiritual and cultural belief system, and the stone heads may have been used as representations of their deities or revered leaders. They could have served as objects of worship or as symbolic representations of spiritual or political power.

30. **(B)** The significance of the Kalinago stone heads lies primarily in providing insights into the artistic skills and craftsmanship of the Kalinago people. These stone carvings showcase the technical and artistic abilities of the Kalinago community in working with stone as a medium. The intricate details and craftsmanship displayed in the stone heads highlight the artistic traditions and techniques of the Kalinago people. They represent a tangible example of their sculptural and carving abilities and provide valuable cultural and historical information. While the stone heads may also have cultural and ceremonial significance within the Kalinago community, such as being used in traditional ceremonies and rituals, their primary importance lies in their artistic and cultural value. They are not primarily used as landmarks for tourist attractions or as a means to highlight the utilization of indigenous materials, although these aspects may contribute to their overall significance.

31. **(A)** Brick was commonly used for the construction of colonial churches and administrative buildings in the Caribbean. The use of brick as a building material was influenced by European colonial architectural styles that were prevalent during the period of colonial rule. Brick offered several advantages for construction in the Caribbean. It provided durability and strength, which was important in areas prone to hurricanes and tropical weather conditions. Brick buildings could withstand the elements better than structures made of materials like timber. Moreover, brick was readily available and could be produced locally using clay and other natural resources found in the region. This made it a practical and cost-effective choice for colonial construction projects. While other materials like concrete, timber, and steel may have been used to some extent, brick was particularly favoured for its suitability to the Caribbean climate and its aesthetic appeal in colonial architecture.

32. **(B)** The primary purpose of art in indigenous societies during the pre-Columbian period was to communicate religious and mythological beliefs. Art served as a visual language through which important cultural, spiritual, and mythological concepts were conveyed. Artworks such as sculptures, pottery, murals, and textiles were often created with a strong emphasis on depicting deities, mythological narratives, and religious rituals. These artworks played a vital role in expressing and preserving the indigenous belief systems, cosmologies, and spiritual practices. Through their artistic creations, indigenous communities expressed their understanding of the divine, their relationship with the natural and supernatural realms, and the stories and legends that shaped their cultural identity. Art served as a means of transmitting and reinforcing their religious and mythological traditions from one generation to another.

33. **(C)** Applique is the most common technique used in Caribbean quilting. Quilting in the Caribbean often involves the layering of different fabric pieces to create a design. Applique is the process of attaching fabric shapes or motifs onto a base fabric, creating a decorative effect. In Caribbean quilting, applique is typically done by hand. Artisans cut out fabric shapes, such as flowers, leaves, animals, or geometric patterns, and stitch them onto a background fabric using various stitching techniques. The appliqued pieces are often layered and stitched down to create a quilted design. This technique allows for the incorporation of vibrant colours, intricate designs, and cultural symbols into the quilts. Caribbean quilting traditions often draw inspiration from the region's diverse cultural heritage, including African, European, and

Indigenous influences. While weaving, embroidery, and macrame are also utilized in Caribbean textile arts, applique stands out as the most commonly used technique in Caribbean quilting.

34. **(A)** Intuitive painting is a style of art that emphasizes spontaneous and instinctive expression rather than formal training or technique. It is a way for artists to tap into their inner thoughts, emotions, and subconscious mind, allowing their creativity to flow freely. In this context, Jessica, who has no formal art training and wishes to explore aspects of her inner self, is the most likely artist to engage in intuitive painting. As someone without formal training, Jessica may not be constrained by conventional rules and techniques, allowing her to explore her creativity and express herself authentically through her artwork. The other options do not align with intuitive painting. John (B), who studied art for several years and wants to appeal to a wide audience, may be more focused on creating work that is commercially successful and may adhere to established techniques and styles. Sam (C), who is self-taught but hopes to develop a commercially viable style of art, may also be more concerned with creating marketable artwork and developing a specific style that resonates with potential buyers. Mary (D), who has years of training but has not yet received critical acclaim for her realistic paintings, may be more inclined to continue refining her technical skills and seeking recognition within the traditional art world.

35. **(D)** Toronto, New York, and London are all known for hosting annual Caribbean festivals. These cities have vibrant Caribbean communities and celebrate Caribbean culture through festivals and events. However, Chicago is not typically recognized as a city known for hosting specific annual Caribbean festivals. While there may be occasional Caribbean-themed events or celebrations in Chicago, it is not as prominent or widely recognized for its Caribbean festivals compared to the other cities mentioned.

36. **(C)** Lithography is a printmaking technique that involves creating an image on a flat surface, typically a stone or metal plate, using oil-based materials. The image is then transferred onto paper or another suitable surface using a press. Lithography allows artists to create prints with a wide range of tonal values, meaning they can achieve various shades of lightness and darkness in the artwork. This is achieved through the use of different types of inks and the manipulation of the printing process. The artist can control the tonal values by adjusting the amount of ink applied and the pressure exerted during printing. This versatility in tonal range is one of the distinguishing features of lithography as a printmaking technique.

37. **(C)** Hector Hyppolite's painting "Damballah La Flambeau" merges human features with mythological representations and exemplifies the syncretic nature of Haitian Vodou. The serpent spirit (loa) with a human face reflects a blend of the spiritual and the earthly elements and demonstrates a strong symbolic and mythological focus rather than abstraction or hyper-realistic depictions.

38. (D) Hyppolite's work often draws from dreamlike and spiritual imagery which aligns with the surrealist movement and emphasizes the subconscious and fantastical elements. The blend of human and mythical features, combined with symbolic representations, shows surrealist influence more than the structured forms of Cubism or the natural focus of realism.

39. (A) Hyppolite's paintings often depicted scenes from Haitian folklore, vodou rituals, and Haitian daily life. His style was characterized by its vibrant colours, intricate details, and a dreamlike quality. He used a combination of bright hues and rich symbolism to create evocative and spiritual imagery. "Damballah La Flambeau" directly represents Damballah, a loa in Vodou, and incorporates symbols and narratives from this spiritual tradition, which are absent in Rastafari (A), Santeria (C), or Revivalism (D).

40. (D) In Haitian art, particularly within Vodou-inspired works, flowers often hold symbolic meaning beyond mere decoration. They frequently represent attributes of deities (loa) in Vodou, highlighting their qualities, powers, or spiritual significance. For example, flowers can evoke a connection to specific spirits, rituals, or aspects of nature that are revered in Haitian spiritual traditions. This symbolic function allows artists like Hector Hyppolite to embed layers of meaning within their paintings. Their presence in "Damballah La Flambeau" is likely intentional to highlight the spiritual connection and attributes associated with Damballah, such as purity, renewal, and fertility.

CAPE®

ART AND DESIGN

PRACTISE TEST 06

Paper 01

1 hour 30 minutes

READ THE FOLLOWING INSTRUCTIONS CAREFULLY.

1. This Practice Test consists of 40 items.

2. You will have 1 hour 30 minutes to answer them.

3. Each item in this Practice Test has four suggested answers lettered (A), (B), (C) and (D). Read each item and decide on the best choice. Look at the sample item below.

Sample Item:

What wax or resist substance is used in batik?

(A) Indigo
(B) Beeswax
(C) Soy wax
(D) Henna

Sample Answer:

The best answer to this item is "Beeswax" and so (B) is shaded.

4. When you are told to begin, turn the page and work as quickly and as carefully as you can. If you cannot answer an item, go on to the next one and return to this item later.

RLF Publications.
"... redefining publishing..."

1. Which of the following female Caribbean artists was renowned for painting colourful portraits of local residents and scenery in Nevis despite her failing eyesight?

(A) Edna Manley
(B) Eva Wilkin
(C) Goldie White
(D) Heather Doram

2. Which of the following articles would have had the greatest value in Maya and Aztec societies?

(A) Gold jewellery
(B) Jade ornaments
(C) Cocoa beans
(D) Cowrie shells

3. Which of the following was the primary material used in pottery in Caribbean indigenous societies?

(A) Clay
(B) Sandstone
(C) Limestone
(D) Bones

4. Which of the following is a paradigm through which art is to be analysed or understood using the approach of the critical theory of art?

I. Social
II. Economic
III. Political
IV. Cultural

(A) I and IV
(B) I, II and IV
(C) I, III and IV
(D) I, II, III and IV

5. Which of the following techniques involves firing pottery at a high temperature in a kiln with a reduced supply of oxygen to create a specific surface effect?

(A) Raku
(B) Pit firing
(C) Sawdust firing
(D) Salt glazing

6. Which of the following is NOT a traditional character or costume worn during Carnival in Trinidad and Tobago?

(A) Annie Palmer
(B) Midnight Robber
(C) Jab Jab
(D) Dame Lorraine

Item 7 refers to the painting below by Pablo Picasso entitled "Girl with a Mandolin."

Image used pursuant to the Creative Commons Licence.
Source: //en.wikipedia.org/wiki/Girl_with_a_Mandolin
(retrieved 30th November 2024)

7. Which of the following artistic styles was utilized by Picasso in painting the above piece?

   (A) Impressionism
   (B) Cubism
   (C) Expressionism
   (D) Fauvism

---

8. What type of housing was provided for enslaved Africans on traditional Caribbean plantations?

   (A) Barracks
   (B) Barracoon
   (C) Cabins
   (D) Huts

9. Which legal framework protects the moral rights of artists?

   (A) Copyright
   (B) Trademark
   (C) Patent
   (D) Registered design

10. How do self-taught artists typically learn their craft?

(A) Through formal art schools and programmes
(B) By studying art history and theory
(C) Through experimentation and trial-and-error
(D) By copying other artists' work

Items 11 to 13 refer to the image below of the Molinere Bay Underwater Sculpture Park located in the Caribbean by British sculptor Jason deCaires Taylor.

Image used pursuant to the Creative Commons Licence
Source:https://commons.wikimedia.org/wiki/File:Underwater_sculptures_at_Molinere_Underwater_Sculpture_Park.jpg (retrieved 30th November 2024)

11. The underwater sculpture park is located in

(A) Barbados
(B) Grenada
(C) St. Kitts and Nevis
(D) Antigua and Barbuda

12. Which of the following is NOT true about the significance of the underwater sculpture as an artistic piece in the Caribbean?

(A) It represents the lost African slaves on the Middle Passage
(B) It is the first underwater sculpture park in the world
(C) It is designed as an artificial coral reef to improve marine life
(D) It is recognized as a World Heritage Site by UNESCO

13. What environmental factor poses a significant challenge to the preservation of underwater sculptures?

(A) Overfishing around the sculptures
(B) Corrosion caused by saline water
(C) Pollution from local industries
(D) Lack of natural light for visibility

14. Which Impressionist artist is known for his series of paintings of water lilies?

(A) Claude Monet
(B) Edgar Degas
(C) Pierre-Auguste Renoir
(D) Camille Pissarro

15. Most European artists who were present in the Caribbean in the pre-emancipation period were commissioned to depict

(A) the cultures of Indigenous people
(B) the families of white planters
(C) the traditions of enslaved people
(D) the landscape of the Caribbean

16. What is the primary characteristic of performance art?

(A) It involves the use of traditional musical instruments
(B) It focuses on storytelling and oral traditions
(C) It emphasizes audience participation and interaction
(D) It explores the use of digital technology and multimedia

17. What was the primary characteristic of a bohio in the pre-Columbian period?

(A) Use of stone as the primary building material
(B) Incorporation of stepped platforms and staircases
(C) Tall pyramid-like structures
(D) Integration of circular or oval shapes in the design

Items 18 to 21 refer to the image below which illustrates a turquoise mask used by Indigenous people in Central America up to the 1500s.

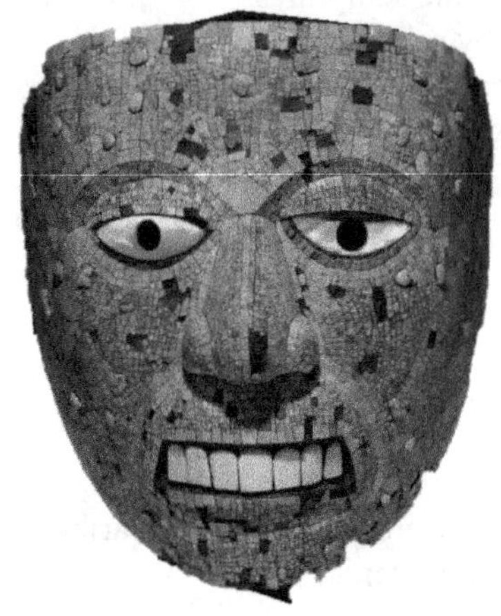

Image © The Trustees of the British Museum (www.britishmusem.org)
Source: https://www.smarthistory.org/turquoise-mosaics-an-introduction/
(retrieved 30th November 2024)

18. The mask depicted was likely associated with which of the following Indigenous groups?

(A) Inca
(B) Garifuna
(C) Aztecs
(D) Kalinago

19. Which of the following techniques was likely used to create the mask?

(A) Tiling
(B) Beadwork
(C) Mosaic
(D) Collage

20. The likely mediums used to create the mask is

(A) wood, shells and glue
(B) bronze, metal and adhesives
(C) stone, pebbles and mortar
(D) paper, sand and dye

21. Which of the following were reasons for mask-wearing in pre-Columbian indigenous societies?

I. To adorn the faces of the dead
II. To commemorate important events
III. To represent deities
IV. To evoke fear during battles

(A) I and II only
(B) I, II and III only
(C) I, III and IV only
(D) I, II, III and IV

22. Which of the following Caribbean islands is known for its African-inspired Carnival costumes and traditions?

(A) Jamaica
(B) Trinidad and Tobago
(C) Bahamas
(D) Dominican Republic

23. Which of the following is a technique used in African art that involves carving a design into a flat surface?

(A) Sgraffito
(B) Relief
(C) Engraving
(D) Incising

24. Which of the following is NOT a common theme in African art?

(A) Landscapes
(B) Portraits of royalty
(C) Mythical creatures
(D) Still lifes

25. Which plant is commonly used to make dyes in Caribbean art?

(A) Indigo
(B) Eucalyptus
(C) Lavender
(D) Peppermint

26. What is the difference between petroglyphs and pictographs?

(A) Petroglyphs are made using paint, while pictographs are made by carving into rock
(B) Petroglyphs depict animals, while pictographs depict humans
(C) Petroglyphs are found indoors, while pictographs are found outdoors
(D) Petroglyphs are made by carving into rock, while pictographs are made using paint

27. What is the term used for the technique of using inanimate objects to create a composition?

(A) Assemblage
(B) Abstraction
(C) Impressionism
(D) Surrealism

28. Which artist is known for his use of inanimate objects in his artworks, such as his "readymades"?

(A) Pablo Picasso
(B) Vincent Van Gogh
(C) Marcel Duchamp
(D) Salvador Dali

29. What animal is commonly associated with parchment paper?

(A) Sheep
(B) Cow
(C) Horse
(D) Pig

30. Which weaving technique is commonly used in the Caribbean to create colourful geometric patterns on textiles?

(A) Tapestry weaving
(B) Twill weaving
(C) Plain weaving
(D) Brocade weaving

31. Which Caribbean country is famous for its murals depicting the revolution and post-revolutionary period?

(A) Cuba
(B) Jamaica
(C) Trinidad and Tobago
(D) Dominican Republic

32. What was the goal of the Caribbean Artists Movement?

(A) To promote European art in the Caribbean
(B) To create a distinct Caribbean art style
(C) To reject all forms of art from the Caribbean
(D) To imitate American art styles

33. What is the process of creating an image by carving it into a block of material, applying ink, and then pressing paper onto the inked surface?

(A) Engraving
(B) Lithography
(C) Woodcut
(D) Serigraphy

34. Which of the following materials is known for its durability and resistance to weathering, making it a popular choice for monument construction in the Caribbean?

(A) Clay
(B) Concrete
(C) Stone
(D) Steel

Items 35 and 36 refer to the photograph below which reflects the famous Devon House Mansion in Kingston, Jamaica.

Photograph used pursuant to the Creative Commons License
Source:https:// //en.wikipedia.org/wiki/Devon_House (retrieved 30th November 2024)

35. Which of the following architectural styles is reflected in the building?

(A) Baroque
(B) Georgian
(C) Romanesque
(D) Gothic

36. Which of the following is a visible feature in the design of the house?

(A) Ribbed vault
(B) Sash window
(C) Flying buttress
(D) Curved walls

37. Which European art movement is characterized by its use of flat, bright colours and bold outlines, often featuring simplified shapes and forms?

(A) Fauvism
(B) Neo-Classicism
(C) Post-Impressionism
(D) Romanticism

38. What does the symbol of the cross in art depicting Haitian Vodou represent?

(A) Christianity and the influence of colonialism
(B) The balance between good and evil
(C) The four cardinal points and elements of the universe
(D) The power and protection of the loas (spirits)

39. Which of the following groups did not have a tradition of body painting in the Caribbean?

(A) European
(B) Asians
(C) Africans
(D) Indigenous people

40. Which of the following is an example of fair use under copyright law?

(A) Selling copies of an artwork without permission from the artist
(B) Using a copyrighted image in a movie without permission from the artist
(C) Critiquing a work of art in a newspaper article
(D) Using someone else's photograph on a website without permission

END OF TEST

ANSWER KEY FOR PRACTICE TEST 06

Item No.	Answer Key
1.	B
2.	B
3.	A
4.	D
5.	A
6.	A
7.	B
8.	A
9.	A
10.	C
11.	B
12.	D
13.	B
14.	A
15.	B
16.	C
17.	D
18.	C
19.	C
20.	A

Item No.	Answer Key
21.	D
22.	B
23.	B
24.	D
25.	A
26.	D
27.	A
28.	C
29.	A
30.	C
31.	A
32.	B
33.	C
34.	C
35.	B
36.	B
37.	A
38.	D
39.	A
40.	C

EXPLANATION FOR PRACTICE TEST 6

1. **(B)** Eva Wilkin was renowned for painting colourful portraits of local residents and scenery in Nevis despite her failing eyesight. She was known for her vibrant and expressive style, capturing the essence and beauty of her subjects and the surrounding environment. Eva Wilkin's artwork celebrated the local culture and landscapes of Nevis, and she is recognized as a significant figure in Caribbean art.

2. **(B)** In Maya and Aztec societies, jade was highly valued and considered a precious stone. It held significant cultural and religious symbolism and was associated with power, status, and divinity. Jade ornaments, such as jewellery, masks, and ceremonial objects, were highly prized and reserved for elite individuals, rulers, and religious ceremonies. The scarcity and labour-intensive process of obtaining and shaping jade made it a highly valuable material in these societies. While gold was also important, it was more readily available than jade which made it less valuable. Cocoa beans and cowrie shells were often used as currencies in these indigenous societies but were not as valuable as jade.

3. **(A)** Clay was the primary material used in pottery in Caribbean indigenous societies. Clay was a natural material that was found in the Caribbean and was easily moulded and shaped when wet. Indigenous communities in the Caribbean often gathered clay from local sources, prepared it by removing impurities, and then shaped it into pottery vessels using techniques such as coiling, slab construction, or moulding. Once the pottery was formed, it would be dried and then fired in a kiln or open fire to harden it into a durable and functional vessel. Clay was an essential material for creating pottery due to its abundance, malleability, and ability to withstand the firing process.

4. **(D)** The critical theory of art encompasses various paradigms through which art can be analysed and understood. These paradigms include the social (I), economic (II), political (III), and cultural (IV) aspects of art. Each of these paradigms offers a different lens through which art can be examined, allowing for a comprehensive understanding of its context and meaning. The social paradigm focuses on the societal and interpersonal dimensions of art, exploring how art reflects and influences social structures, relationships, and norms. The economic paradigm examines the economic factors related to art, such as the art market, commodification, and the role of art in economic systems. The political paradigm analyses the political dimensions of art, including power dynamics, resistance, and the role of art in shaping and challenging political ideologies. The cultural paradigm explores the cultural aspects of art, including cultural identity, symbolism, and how art reflects and shapes cultural values and beliefs.

5. **(A)** Raku is a pottery technique that involves firing pottery at a low temperature and then removing the pieces from the kiln while they are still hot. The pottery is then placed in a combustible material, such as sawdust or leaves, which creates a reduced atmosphere. This reduction process affects the glazes and surface effects, resulting in unique and unpredictable patterns and colours on the pottery. Salt glazing (D), on the other hand, involves firing pottery with the introduction of salt into the kiln to create a glaze, as mentioned earlier. Pit firing (B) and sawdust firing (C) are alternative methods

of firing pottery, but they do not involve the specific surface effect achieved through the reduction atmosphere in Raku firing.

6. **(A)** Annie Palmer is not a traditional character or costume worn during Carnival in Trinidad and Tobago. She is actually a historical figure associated with Rose Hall Great House in Jamaica and the subject of local legends and stories. On the other hand, Midnight Robber (B), Jab Jab (C), and Dame Lorraine (D) are traditional characters and costumes commonly seen during Carnival in Trinidad and Tobago.

7. **(B)** Picasso used the artistic style of Cubism in most of his paintings. Cubism, which emerged in the early 20th Century, was a revolutionary art movement that transformed the way artists represented and perceived reality. It was heavily influenced by African and other non-Western art forms, particularly the aesthetic qualities of African masks and sculptures. African art played a significant role in shaping the visual language of Cubism. Artists such as Pablo Picasso and Georges Braque were inspired by the geometric forms, simplified shapes, and expressive power found in African masks and sculptures. They admired the abstract and conceptual approach to representing the human figure in African art, which challenged the naturalistic conventions of European art at the time. In Cubism, artists sought to depict objects from multiple viewpoints, fracturing and reassembling them in geometric forms and facets. This approach emphasized the subjectivity of perception and broke away from the traditional notions of representation in European art. By incorporating elements of African art, Cubism aimed to explore new ways of seeing and representing the world, rejecting the conventional perspective and seeking a more abstract and fragmented representation.

8. **(A)** Enslaved people on traditional Caribbean plantations were often provided with barracks as their housing. Barracks were large, communal buildings divided into smaller compartments or rooms where enslaved individuals or families were assigned to live. These barracks were typically basic and crowded, with little privacy or comfort. They were designed to accommodate a significant number of enslaved people and were meant to be cost-effective for plantation owners.

9. **(A)** Copyright is a legal framework that grants creators, including artists, the exclusive rights to their original works. These rights include the right to reproduce, distribute, display, and perform the work. Additionally, copyright law also protects the moral rights of artists, which are non-economic rights that reflect the personal and reputational connection between the artist and their work. Moral rights generally include the right of attribution (the right to be recognized as the creator of the work), the right to integrity (the right to protect the work from distortion, mutilation, or modification that could harm the artist's reputation), and the right to disclosure (the right to determine when and how the work is made available to the public).

10. **(C)** Self-taught artists typically learn their craft through experimentation and trial and error. Unlike artists who receive formal training through art schools and programmes (A), self-taught artists pursue their artistic development independently. They often rely on their own curiosity, creativity, and passion to explore different techniques, materials, and subject matters. Through a process of experimentation and trial and error, they learn and refine their artistic skills. While studying art history and theory

(B) can certainly be beneficial for self-taught artists to expand their knowledge and understanding of the art world, it is not a necessary or exclusive means of learning their craft. Additionally, copying other artists' work (D) can be a part of the learning process for some artists, including self-taught ones, as it allows them to study and understand different styles and techniques. However, it is important to note that simply copying others' work is not the sole or preferred method of learning for self-taught artists. They often strive to develop their own unique artistic voice and style through personal exploration and experimentation.

11. **(B)** The Molinere Bay Underwater Sculpture Park is located in Grenada. It is an underwater art gallery that features a collection of submerged sculptures created by British artist Jason deCaires Taylor. The sculptures are positioned on the ocean floor and serve as an artificial reef, attracting marine life and providing a unique environment for divers and snorkelers to explore. The sculptures in the park are made from environmentally friendly materials that promote the growth of coral and marine organisms. Over time, the sculptures become covered in colourful corals and transformed by the marine ecosystem. The park combines art and conservation, offering a visually stunning and educational experience for visitors while also contributing to the preservation of marine life and the promotion of sustainable tourism. The park has gained international recognition and has become a popular attraction for tourists and art enthusiasts. It offers a unique perspective on art, blurring the lines between human creation and the natural world, and highlighting the interconnectedness between art, the environment, and marine ecosystems.

12. **(D)** While the Molinere Bay Underwater Sculpture Park is an impressive and unique artistic creation, it is not recognized as a World Heritage Site by UNESCO to date. The park has gained recognition and popularity for its innovative approach to combining art and marine conservation, but it has not received the designation of a World Heritage Site.

13. **(B)** The underwater sculptures in Grenada face significant challenges due to the saline water environment, which accelerates the corrosion and degradation of the materials used in their construction. Saltwater is highly corrosive, especially to metals and certain non-durable materials, causing gradual wear and tear over time. This natural process necessitates regular maintenance to preserve the sculptures, which can be costly and logistically challenging. Additionally, marine growth like algae and barnacles, while adding to the sculptures' ecological integration, can obscure the details of the artwork, further diminishing their visual appeal. These factors limit the longevity and aesthetic preservation of the sculptures, making maintenance a critical aspect of their upkeep.

14. **(A)** Claude Monet, a renowned French painter, is famous for his extensive series of paintings depicting water lilies and the surrounding landscapes. His "Water Lilies" series, created towards the end of his career, showcases his mastery of capturing the play of light, colour, and reflections on the water's surface. Monet's water lilies paintings are considered iconic examples of impressionist art.

15. **(B)** Most European artists who were present in the Caribbean in the pre-emancipation period were primarily commissioned to depict the families of white planters. During the pre-emancipation period in the Caribbean, European artists were often commissioned by wealthy white planters, plantation owners, and colonial officials to create portraits and scenes that portrayed their families, status, and the opulence of their lifestyles. These commissioned artworks typically depicted the privileged European elite rather than focusing on the cultures of indigenous people, the traditions of enslaved people, or the landscape of the Caribbean.

16. **(C)** Performance art is a form of artistic expression in which the artist creates a live-action event that involves the audience in some way. It goes beyond traditional art mediums and can incorporate elements of theatre, dance, music, and other forms of creative expression. Audience participation and interaction are key components of performance art, as it often seeks to create a shared experience between the artist and the viewers, blurring the boundaries between the artwork and its audience.

17. **(D)** A bohio was a traditional dwelling structure found in the Taino societies during the pre-Columbian period. It was characterized by its circular or oval shape, often constructed using natural materials such as wood, thatch, and palm leaves. The circular or oval shape allowed for efficient use of materials and provided structural stability. The design of bohios varied across different Indigenous groups, but the integration of circular or oval shapes was a common characteristic.

18. **(C)** The information provided is that the mask was used by indigenous people in Central America. Based on the options, the only answer can be the Aztecs since they settled in Central America in the pre-Columbian era, especially in the region that is now present-day Mexico. The Aztecs were known for their rich cultural traditions and artistic expressions, including the creation of intricate masks. The turquoise mask shown in the image is consistent with the artistic style and materials used by the Aztecs in their masks and other ceremonial objects. The Inca (A) settled in South America (primarily in the region that is modern-day Peru). The Garifuna (B) and Kalinago (D) settled on the islands in the Caribbean.

19. **(C)** The mask depicted in the image appears to be made of small, carefully arranged pieces of turquoise stone or material, forming a mosaic-like pattern. Mosaic is a technique where small pieces of materials, such as stone, glass, or tile, are arranged and set into a surface to create a design or image. In this case, the use of turquoise pieces in a mosaic pattern gives the mask its distinctive appearance.

20. **(A)** Given the nature of mask-making in Aztec societies, it is likely that the mediums used to create the mask were wood, shells, and glue. Wood is often used as a base material for masks, providing a solid structure for carving and shaping. Shells can be used to decorate the mask, adding texture and visual interest. Glue or adhesive substances would be used to secure the various elements together, such as attaching the shells to the wooden base.

21. **(D)** Items I, II, III, and IV were all reasons for mask-wearing in pre-Columbian indigenous societies. Masks held significant cultural and ritual importance in pre-Columbian indigenous societies. They were often used as part of funerary rituals, particularly to adorn the faces of the dead. Additionally, they were often worn during ceremonies to celebrate significant milestones or historical events. Furthermore, masks were essential in religious ceremonies and were sometimes used to embody divine beings or spiritual entities. Finally, they were used to intimidate enemies in warfare.

22. **(B)** Trinidad and Tobago is known for its vibrant and elaborate Carnival celebrations, which include African-inspired costumes, music, and traditions. The Carnival in Trinidad and Tobago is one of the most famous and culturally significant festivals in the Caribbean region. African traditions and customs have played a significant role in shaping the Carnival celebrations in Trinidad and Tobago. The African diaspora brought to the Caribbean through the transatlantic slave trade, has left a lasting impact on the cultural landscape of the region. Many of the Carnival costumes, music, and dances in Trinidad and Tobago draw inspiration from African traditions. During Carnival, participants don elaborate and flamboyant costumes that often incorporate African-inspired designs, fabrics, and motifs. These costumes are meticulously crafted with vibrant colours, feathers, beads, and other embellishments. They reflect the rich cultural heritage and pay homage to the African roots of the Trinidadian and Tobagonian people.

23. **(B)** Relief carving is a technique used in African art where the design is carved or sculpted to create a raised surface on a flat background. The artist carves away the surrounding material, leaving the design or figure raised above the surface. This technique is commonly used in African sculptures, masks, and other forms of art. The raised areas can vary in depth, creating a sense of depth and three-dimensionality to the artwork. Relief carving allows for intricate detailing and the depiction of figures, symbols, and scenes. Options (A), (C) and (D), while used in African art, are not exclusive to African art.

24. **(D)** Still lifes, which typically depict inanimate objects such as fruits, flowers, or everyday items arranged in a composition, are not a common theme in traditional African art. African art has a strong focus on human figures, portraits, masks, sculptures, and representations of animals, as well as themes related to spirituality, mythology, ancestral beliefs, rituals, and cultural traditions. Hence, landscapes (A), portraits of royalty (B), and mythical creatures (C) are common themes in African art. Overall, African art often reflects the human experience, cultural practices, and connections to the natural and spiritual realms, rather than the depiction of static objects in a still-life arrangement.

25. **(A)** Indigo is a plant commonly used to make dyes in Caribbean art. The leaves of the indigo plant contain a blue pigment that can be extracted and used to create various shades of blue dye. The dyeing process often involves fermenting the leaves to release the pigment and then immersing the fabric or material in the dye bath to achieve the desired colour. Indigo dye has been used for centuries in many cultures, including the

Caribbean, to colour textiles, garments, and other artistic creations. It is known for its rich blue hue and its significance in traditional and cultural practices.

26. **(D)** Petroglyphs and pictographs are both forms of rock art created by ancient cultures, but they differ in their method of creation. Petroglyphs are images or designs that are carved, chiselled, or incised into the surface of rock. This is typically done by using tools to remove layers of the rock and reveal the desired image. Petroglyphs often feature deep grooves and distinctive carvings, that can withstand the test of time. On the other hand, pictographs are images or designs that are painted or drawn onto the surface of rock using pigments or dyes. Pictographs can be created by applying paint directly to the rock surface or by using brushes, fingers, or other tools to apply the pigment.

27. **(A)** Assemblage is the term used for the technique of creating a composition by assembling or combining various inanimate objects, often found or recycled materials, into a cohesive artwork. It involves arranging and manipulating objects in a deliberate manner to create a visually appealing or conceptually meaningful composition. Assemblage artworks can include a wide range of materials such as everyday objects, scrap metal, wood, fabric, paper, and more. Artists who work with assemblage often use these objects to convey a specific theme, idea, or message through the combination and juxtaposition of different elements. Abstraction (B), Impressionism (C), and Surrealism (D) are different artistic styles or movements that focus on other aspects of artistic expression and representation. Abstraction emphasizes the use of non-representational or non-objective forms and shapes. Impressionism is characterized by capturing the fleeting impressions of light and colour in a scene. Surrealism explores the realm of dreams, the subconscious, and irrational juxtapositions in art.

28. **(C)** Marcel Duchamp is known for his innovative and provocative approach to art, particularly through his use of "readymades." Readymades are ordinary objects that Duchamp selected and designated as artworks simply by presenting them in the context of an art gallery. These objects were often mass-produced and already existing, such as a urinal titled "Fountain" or a bicycle wheel mounted on a stool. Duchamp's use of readymades challenged traditional notions of art and raised questions about the role of the artist, the definition of art, and the concept of originality. By selecting and presenting everyday objects as art, Duchamp blurred the boundaries between art and everyday life, emphasizing the idea or concept behind the artwork rather than its aesthetic qualities. Pablo Picasso (A), Vincent Van Gogh (B), and Salvador Dali (D) were influential artists in their own right, but they are not specifically known for their use of inanimate objects or readymades in the same way as Marcel Duchamp.

29. **(A)** Parchment paper is commonly made from sheepskin. The skin of sheep is processed and treated to create a smooth and durable material that is suitable for writing, drawing, or other artistic purposes. The process involves removing the hair from the sheepskin and then stretching and drying it to create a thin, translucent sheet of parchment. Sheepskin is preferred for making parchment paper because of its quality and suitability for writing and drawing. The use of sheepskin for parchment

paper has a long history and is still practised today, although modern alternatives made from plant-based materials are also available.

30. (C) Plain weaving, also known as tabby weaving or basketweave, is a simple and common weaving technique characterized by its regular and straightforward interlacing of warp and weft threads. It involves passing the weft thread over and under the warp threads in a repetitive pattern. This technique is often used to create textiles with vibrant geometric patterns by using different coloured yarns in the warp and weft, resulting in a visually appealing and intricate design. While other weaving techniques such as tapestry weaving (A), twill weaving (B), and brocade weaving (D) are also practised in the Caribbean and around the world, plain weaving is particularly recognized for its widespread use and popularity in creating colourful geometric patterns on textiles in the region.

31. (A) Cuba is famous for its murals depicting the revolution and post-revolutionary period. After the Cuban Revolution in 1959, murals became an important form of artistic expression in Cuba, particularly in Havana. These murals often depict scenes from the revolution, historical events, political figures, and social themes. The murals serve as visual representations of Cuba's revolutionary spirit and its commitment to social justice and equality. They have become an integral part of the country's cultural and artistic landscape.

32. (B) The Caribbean Artists Movement (CAM) emerged in the 1960s as a collective of Caribbean artists, writers, and intellectuals who aimed to explore and promote Caribbean identity and culture through various art forms. They sought to establish a unique artistic expression that reflected the diverse experiences and heritage of the Caribbean region. The movement aimed to challenge the dominance of European art and to create a platform for Caribbean artists to showcase their own perspectives, histories, and narratives. Through their work, the members of the Caribbean Artists Movement aimed to assert the cultural independence and vitality of the Caribbean art scene.

33. (C) The process of creating an image by carving it into a block of material, applying ink, and then pressing paper onto the inked surface is called a woodcut. Woodcut is a printmaking technique that involves carving a design into a block of wood, leaving the raised areas that will hold ink. The ink is then applied to the surface of the block, and paper or fabric is pressed onto it, transferring the inked design onto the paper. Woodcut is a traditional and widely used technique in printmaking, known for its distinctive and often bold and expressive qualities. The other techniques can be distinguished. Engraving (A) is a printmaking technique where an image is incised or engraved into a hard surface, typically metal, using a sharp tool called a burin. The incised lines are then inked, and the surface is wiped clean, leaving ink only in the engraved lines. Paper is then pressed onto the inked surface, transferring the image onto the paper. Engraving is known for its fine and detailed lines. Lithography (B) is a printmaking technique based on the principle that oil and water repel each other. The image is drawn or painted on a smooth surface (typically a lithographic stone or a metal plate) using an oil-based medium. Then, the surface is dampened with water, which is repelled by the oily image areas. Ink is applied to the surface, adhering to the oily image and repelled by the wet areas. The image is then transferred to paper or another material using a press. Serigraphy (D), also known as screen printing, is a printmaking technique where ink is forced through a fine mesh screen onto a surface to create an image. The screen is prepared by blocking out areas that are not part of the image, leaving open areas for the ink to pass through. Ink is applied to one side of the screen, and a squeegee is used to push the ink through the open areas of the screen onto the printing surface, such as paper or fabric. Serigraphy allows for vibrant and opaque prints and is commonly used in commercial printing and for creating posters and apparel.

34. **(C)** Stone is known for its durability and resistance to weathering, which makes it a popular choice for monument construction in the Caribbean and many other regions. Stone monuments can withstand the effects of wind, rain, and other environmental factors, allowing them to retain their structural integrity and visual appeal over time. Additionally, stone offers a natural and timeless aesthetic that adds to the cultural and historical significance of monuments. Various types of stone, such as limestone, granite, and sandstone, have been used for constructing monuments in the Caribbean due to their strength and longevity.

35. **(B)** The Devon House Mansion exhibits characteristics of the Georgian architectural style. The Georgian style emerged during the reigns of the British monarchs George I to George IV (1714-1830) and was widely influential in colonial British architecture, including in Jamaica. Georgian architecture is characterized by symmetrical designs, proportioned facades, classical elements such as columns and pediments, and a sense of elegance and symmetry. The Devon House Mansion features these characteristics, including a symmetrical facade, large sash windows, a central entrance, and classical elements in its detailing.

36. **(B)** Sash windows are a prominent feature in the design of the Devon House Mansion. Sash windows are characterized by one or more movable panels or sashes, that can be vertically slid open or closed within the window frame. They are typically divided into multiple smaller panes of glass, known as "lights," held together by wooden glazing bars. Sash windows became popular during the Georgian era and are commonly associated with buildings of that period. The Devon House Mansion showcases these distinctive sash windows, which contribute to the overall architectural style and aesthetic of the building.

37. **(A)** Fauvism is the European art movement characterized by its use of flat, bright colours and bold outlines, often featuring simplified shapes and forms. Fauvist artists sought to express their subjective experiences and emotions through intense and non-naturalistic colours. They deliberately used bold and arbitrary colour choices, emphasizing the expressive potential of colour rather than realistic representation. Fauvism emerged in the early 20th Century and had a significant influence on the development of modern art.

38. (D) Vodou is a syncretic religion that incorporates elements of African, Indigenous, and Christian beliefs and practices. One of the most common interpretations of the cross in art depicting Haitian Vodou is the power and protection of the loas (spirits). Indeed, the cross symbol in Haitian Vodou often represents the connection between the human world and the spiritual realm. It is associated with the presence and power of the loas, which are the spirits or deities in Vodou. The cross can serve as a focal point for communication and invocation of these spirits, as well as a symbol of their presence and protection.

39. (A) Europeans did not have a tradition of body painting in the Caribbean. Body painting has been a cultural practice among various Indigenous peoples, Africans, and Asians in the Caribbean region. Indigenous peoples in the Caribbean, such as the Taino and Caribs, had a long history of body painting for various purposes including rituals, ceremonies, and adornment. African cultures brought to the Caribbean through the transatlantic slave trade also had rich traditions of body painting and scarification. Similarly, Asian cultures, particularly those from the Indian subcontinent, have practices such as mehndi (henna body art) that involve intricate designs applied to the skin. However, European cultural traditions generally did not include body painting as a prominent practice in the Caribbean.

40. (C) Under copyright law, fair use is a legal doctrine that allows for the limited use of copyrighted material without permission from the copyright holder. Fair use is typically determined by considering factors such as the purpose and character of the use, the nature of the copyrighted work, the amount and substantiality of the portion used, and the effect of the use on the potential market for the original work. Options (A), (B) and (D) would generally not qualify as fair use as they involve using copyrighted material without authorization for commercial purposes or without transforming the original work in a significant way. On the other hand, critiquing a work of art in a newspaper article is often considered a transformative use and falls within the scope of fair use. Commentary, criticism, and review are generally recognized as fair use purposes, allowing for the use of copyrighted material to support and enhance the critique or analysis of the work.

CAPE®

ART AND DESIGN

PRACTICE TEST 07

Paper 01

1 hour 30 minutes

READ THE FOLLOWING INSTRUCTIONS CAREFULLY.

1. This Mock Examination consists of 40 items.

2. You will have 1 hour 30 minutes to answer them.

3. Each item in this Mock Examination has four suggested answers lettered (A), (B), (C) and (D). Read each item and decide on the best choice. Look at the sample item below.

Sample Item:

Which Afro-Cuban religion heavily influenced the art of Belkis Ayón?

(A) Santería
(B) Abakuá
(C) Comfa
(D) Ifá

Sample Answer:

(A)   

The best answer to this item is "Abakuá" and so (B) is shaded.

4. When you are told to begin, turn the page and work as quickly and as carefully as you can. If you cannot answer an item, go on to the next one and return to this item later.

RLF Publications.
"... redefining publishing..."

1. Which of the following BEST describes iconography in art?

(A) The study of icons and symbols in art
(B) The creation of digital icons for websites
(C) The use of icons to represent popular cultural figures
(D) The use of colours to create a visual hierarchy in design

2. In art, what is the significance of a recurring image or symbol?

(A) It represents the artist's signature style
(B) It indicates the subject matter of the artwork
(C) It adds depth and meaning to the artwork
(D) It has no significant meaning

3. Which of the following is a characteristic of Gothic stained-glass windows?

(A) Simple geometric designs
(B) Minimal use of colour
(C) Symmetrical composition
(D) Elaborate storytelling scenes

4. Which Caribbean island has a famous Gothic-style clock tower?

(A) Antigua
(B) St. Kitts and Nevis
(C) Dominica
(D) Grenada

5. Which of the following UNESCO sites is located in Haiti?

(A) Morne Trois Pitons National Park
(B) Brimstone Hill Fortress National Park
(C) Blue and John Crow Mountains National Park
(D) National History Park – Citadel, Sans Souci, Ramiers

6. Which European art movement is known for its use of geometric shapes and primary colours?

(A) Baroque
(B) Rococo
(C) Cubism
(D) Romanticism

7. Which of the following is a common architectural feature found in Mayan cities?

(A) Spires
(B) Domes
(C) Arches
(D) Corbel vaults

8. What is the meaning behind the use of the conch shell in Caribbean iconography?

(A) Communication and expression
(B) Protection and safety
(C) Spiritual awakening and enlightenment
(D) Healing and renewal

9. What is the term for the unauthorized use of someone else's work in a way that violates the owner's legal rights?

(A) Piracy
(B) Plagiarism
(C) Infringement
(D) Theft

Items 10 to 13 refer to the image below which is a replica of Edna Manley's Negro Aroused sculpture.

Image used pursuant to the Creative Commons Licence
Source: https://commons.wikimedia.org/wiki/File:Negro_Aroused_on_waterfront.jpg
(retrieved 30th November 2024)

10. Which of the following is the BEST description of the replicated sculpture?

(A) Cenotaph
(B) Monument
(C) Epitaph
(D) Memorial

11. The replicated sculpture, as depicted, is made of bronze. The original sculpture is likely made from

(A) wood
(B) stone
(C) metal
(D) glass

12. The technique used for the replication of the original art is referred to as

(A) exaggeration
(B) scaling
(C) balancing
(D) casting

13. The primary message of the sculpture is

(A) the celebration of Caribbean culture and heritage
(B) the depiction of the struggle for racial equality
(C) the exploration of gender and sexuality
(D) the critique of colonialism institutions

14. Which of the following national dresses is NOT correctly paired with its Caribbean country?

(A) Jamaica --- Quadrille
(B) Antigua and Barbuda --- Karabela
(C) Grenada --- Jupe
(D) Guyana --- Dashikis

---

15. Which of the following materials would be most appealing to an intuitive artist in the Caribbean?

(A) Marble and stone
(B) Metal and glass
(C) Recycled materials and objects
(D) Paints and canvases

16. Which art movement was influenced by the Industrial Revolution?

(A) Art Deco
(B) Romanticism
(C) Realism
(D) Abstract Expressionism

17. What type of painting is Hector Hyppolite known for?

(A) Realism
(B) Impressionism
(C) Surrealism
(D) Abstract

18. The Edna Manley College of the Visual and Performing Arts was established in

(A) 1944
(B) 1965
(C) 1995
(D) 2010

19. What was the role of music in Caribbean enslaved communities?

(A) It was used primarily for entertainment
(B) It was used as a form of communication and resistance
(C) It was discouraged by slave owners
(D) It was only practised by the wealthy elite

20. Which of the following is NOT a contemporary technological technique used in art?

(A) Augmented reality
(B) Virtual reality
(C) Oil painting
(D) Digital printing

21. What was the primary function of the pottery utensils created by indigenous Caribbean peoples?

(A) Cooking and food storage
(B) Religious ceremonies
(C) Decorative purposes
(D) Trade and commerce

22. Canute Caliste's intuitive paintings often depict scenes from everyday life in Carriacou, Grenada. What important theme is the most prominent in his artwork?

(A) Mythological creatures and folklore
(B) Abstract interpretations of nature
(C) Religious symbolism and rituals
(D) Historical events and political activism

23. Which Jewish community is associated with the Jewish cemetery in Barbados?

(A) Sephardic Jews
(B) Ashkenazi Jews
(C) Mizrahi Jews
(D) Beta Israel Jews

Items 24 to 28 refer to the image below which represents a Hindu sculpture in the Caribbean.

Source: http://www.caribbean-sun.com/img/berichte/bericht_58/pic1.jpg (accessed November 2024)

24. The likely location of the depicted sculpture is

(A) St. Vincent
(B) Trinidad
(C) Jamaica
(D) Barbados

25. The sculpture is associated with a

(A) mandir
(B) synagogue
(C) church
(D) mosque

26. Which of the following historical events in the Caribbean could account for the significance attached to the sculpture?

(A) Colonialism
(B) Indentureship
(C) Plantation slavery
(D) Independence

27. Which of the following architectural styles, derived from India, was used to create the sculpture depicted in the diagram?

(A) Dravidian
(B) Nagara
(C) Mughal
(D) Vernacular

28. The sculpture is red in colour. Which of the following is the BEST symbolism of red?

(A) Passion and love
(B) Strength and bravery
(C) Happiness and hope
(D) Abundance and nature

---

29. The presence of a midden is usually a sign of a/an

(A) human occupation
(B) archaeological excavation
(C) collapsed civilization
(D) demographic transition

30. Which of the following BEST describes intuitive art?

(A) Art that is created with conscious planning and intention
(B) Art that is created through a process of deep introspection and self-reflection
(C) Art that is created using non-traditional materials and found objects
(D) Art that is created through a spontaneous and unstructured approach

31. Which is the MOST associated with batik art in the Caribbean?

(A) Wood
(B) Silk
(C) Cotton
(D) Polyester

32. The MOST likely technique used to make crochets in the Caribbean is

(A) looping
(B) knitting
(C) embroidery
(D) applique

33. What is the process of weaving where the weft thread is wrapped around the warp thread and then woven back called?

(A) Tapestry
(B) Brocade
(C) Jacquard
(D) Dobby

34. Which of the following is NOT a traditional use of body painting in various cultures?

(A) Spiritual and religious purposes
(B) Camouflage for hunting
(C) Celebratory occasions
(D) Medical treatments

Items 35 and 36 refer to the image of a bowl in the Maya culture which has a serpent on its exterior.

Image is in the public domain.
Source: https://www.metmuseum.org/art/collection/search/318405
(retreived 30th November 2024)

35. The medium of the bowl is likely

(A) stone
(B) ceramic
(C) wood
(D) basalt

36. What methods might have been employed by the Mayans to make the serpent the surface of the bowl?

I. Sgraffito
II. Craving
III. Firing
IV. Incising

(A) I and II
(B) II and IV
(C) II and III
(D) III and IV

37. All of the following are features of impressionism EXCEPT

(A) Small, visible brushstrokes
(B) Unblended colours
(C) Accurate depiction of naïve light
(D) Fragmented and abstracted shapes

38. Elizabeth is skilled in batik art. She is likely working with

(A) paint and canvas
(B) dye and fabric
(C) knitting needles and yarn
(D) glue and paper

39. Which of the following is NOT a step in the art criticism process?

(A) Description
(B) Analysis
(C) Evaluation
(D) Appreciation

40. What is the difference between formalism and contextualism in art criticism?

(A) Formalism focuses on the physical qualities of the artwork, while contextualism considers the artwork's historical and social context
(B) Formalism is an intangible aspect of art, while contextualism is a tangible aspect of art
(C) Formalism considers the purpose of the art, while contextualism considers the use of the art
(D) Formalism refers to the procedure used to create art, while contextualism refers to how the art is viewed after it is created

END OF TEST

ANSWER KEY FOR PRACTICE TEST 07

Item No.	Answer Key
1.	A
2.	C
3.	D
4.	B
5.	D
6.	C
7.	D
8.	C
9.	C
10.	B
11.	A
12.	B
13.	B
14.	B
15.	C
16.	C
17.	C
18.	C
19.	B
20.	C

Item No.	Answer Key
21.	A
22.	B
23.	A
24.	B
25.	A
26.	B
27.	A
28.	B
29.	A
30.	D
31.	C
32.	A
33.	A
34.	D
35.	B
36.	B
37.	D
38.	B
39.	D
40.	A

EXPLANATIONS TO ANSWERS FOR PRACTICE TEST 07

1. **(A)** Iconography in art refers to the study and interpretation of visual symbols, motifs, and icons within artworks. It involves analysing the meaning, significance, and cultural context of these symbols and how they contribute to the overall message and narrative of the artwork. Iconography can encompass a wide range of elements, including religious symbols, mythological figures, allegorical representations, and cultural references. Through iconography, art historians and scholars can delve into the deeper meanings and cultural associations embedded within artworks, providing insights into the artist's intentions and the broader social and historical context in which the art was created.

2. **(C)** When a recurring image or symbol appears in an artwork, it often carries significance and contributes to the overall meaning and interpretation of the piece. These recurring images can function as visual motifs or symbols that convey deeper themes, ideas, or emotions. They can create a sense of visual unity and coherence within the artwork, establishing connections and associations between different elements. The repetition of an image or symbol can evoke a sense of emphasis, inviting viewers to pay closer attention to its presence and consider its implications. Additionally, recurring images or symbols can serve as visual cues, providing a visual language through which the artist communicates their intentions, messages, or narratives. By repeating certain images or symbols throughout their work, artists can engage viewers in a dialogue, provoke thought, and invite multiple layers of interpretation.

3. **(D)** One of the characteristic features of Gothic stained-glass windows is the use of elaborate storytelling scenes. Gothic stained glass is known for its narrative quality, where intricate and detailed scenes are depicted within the glass panels. These scenes often portray biblical stories, saints, martyrs, and other religious or historical events. The purpose of these elaborate designs was to educate and inspire the viewers, as well as to enhance the spiritual atmosphere of the space. The scenes were carefully crafted using vibrant colours, intricate patterns, and delicate details to bring the narratives to life. While simple geometric designs and symmetrical compositions can also be found in Gothic stained glass, the prominent characteristic is the use of storytelling scenes to convey religious or historical narratives.

4. **(B)** St. Kitts and Nevis is known for having a famous Gothic-style clock tower. The clock tower is located in the capital city of Basseterre on the island of St. Kitts. It is a prominent architectural feature and a popular tourist attraction in the area. The Gothic style of the clock tower is characterized by its pointed arches, intricate detailing, and vertical emphasis. This architectural style is reminiscent of the Gothic architecture that originated in medieval Europe and is often associated with grand cathedrals and other religious structures.

5. **(D)** The National History Park - Citadel, Sans Souci, Ramiers is located in Haiti. It is a UNESCO World Heritage site and encompasses the historic buildings of Sans Souci Palace, Ramiers Fortress, and the Citadel of Henry Christophe. These structures are significant historical landmarks and represent Haiti's rich history and architectural heritage. The Citadel, in particular, is a renowned fortress and is considered one of the largest fortifications in the Americas. The other options are not located in Haiti. The Morne Trois Pitons National Park (A) is located in Dominica. The Brimstone Hill Fortress National Park (B) is located in St. Kitts and Nevis. The Blue and John Crow Mountains National Park (C) is located in Jamaica. These sites, although not located in Haiti, are notable UNESCO World Heritage sites in their respective countries, each with its own unique cultural, historical, and natural significance.

6. **(C)** Cubism was an influential European art movement that emerged in the early 20th Century, pioneered by artists Pablo Picasso and Georges Braque. It is known for its use of geometric shapes, fragmented forms, and the exploration of multiple viewpoints in a single composition. Cubist artworks often depict objects from multiple angles simultaneously, breaking them down into geometric shapes such as cubes, cones, and spheres. Primary colours, which are the basic colours of red, blue, and yellow, were commonly used in Cubist artworks to create bold and vibrant compositions. The movement aimed to challenge traditional notions of perspective and representation, emphasizing the abstract and conceptual aspects of art. Baroque (A) and Rococo (B) are art movements from a different period, known for their ornate and decorative styles. Romanticism (D), on the other hand, focused on emotional expression and individual experiences, often featuring dramatic and sublime subject matter.

7. **(D)** Corbel vaults are a common architectural feature found in Mayan cities. They are a construction technique used to create roof structures and vaulted ceilings. In this technique, stones or other building materials are stacked in horizontal layers, each one projecting slightly inward until they meet at the top, forming a vaulted shape. The corbel vaults in Mayan architecture were typically made of stone and were used to cover large interior spaces, such as temples and palaces. While spires (A), domes (B), and arches (C) are architectural features that can be found in other architectural styles, such as Gothic or Romanesque, they are not typically associated with Mayan architecture. Mayan architecture is characterized by its unique style and features, including the use of corbel vaults, intricate carvings, and stepped pyramids.

8. **(C)** In Caribbean cultures, the conch shell is often regarded as a sacred object with spiritual significance. It is associated with the idea of spiritual awakening, enlightenment, and divine communication. The conch shell's spiral shape is seen as a symbol of spiritual growth, transformation, and the journey towards higher consciousness. In rituals and ceremonies, the conch shell may be blown to invoke the presence of deities or spirits, and its sound is believed to carry spiritual energy and messages. It is also used as a ritual instrument to call for attention, create sacred space, and signal important moments during spiritual practices.

9. **(C)** Infringement refers to the act of using, reproducing, distributing, displaying, or modifying someone else's copyrighted work without obtaining the necessary permission or license from the copyright owner. It involves the violation of the exclusive rights granted to the creator of the original work, such as the right to reproduce, distribute, publicly display, or create derivative works based on the original. Piracy (A) and theft (D) are sometimes used colloquially to describe infringement, but in a legal context, infringement is the more accurate term. Plagiarism (B), on the other hand, refers specifically to the act of presenting someone else's work, ideas, or words as one's own without giving proper credit, and is often associated with academic or literary contexts rather than legal violations.

10. **(B)** The replicated sculpture is best described as a monument. A monument is a structure, sculpture, or memorial that is created to commemorate a person, event, or significant historical or cultural significance. Monuments are typically designed to be permanent and serve as a visual representation of remembrance, tribute, or celebration. In the case of the replicated sculpture of Edna Manley's Negro Aroused, it is intended to honour and commemorate the original artwork created by the artist. The sculpture is a notable and enduring representation of Manley's artistic expression and contribution to Caribbean art. The other options can be distinguished and do not accurately describe the replicated sculpture in question. A cenotaph (A) is a monument or structure that is erected in honour of a person or group of people whose remains are elsewhere. It serves as a memorial or tribute to individuals who may not be buried at the site. An epitaph (C) is a brief inscription or statement that is typically written on a tombstone or monument to honour and remember a deceased person. It is usually a commemorative message or tribute to the individual buried at the site. A memorial (D) is a structure, monument, or object that is created to honour and remember a person, group, or event. Memorials are often built to commemorate significant historical events, individuals, or tragedies. They serve as a means of remembrance and tribute.

11. **(A)** The likely medium for the original sculpture is wood. This is because Edna Manley is renowned for the use of local wood from Jamaica in the creation of her sculptures. She did not use stone (B), metal (C) or glass (D).

12. **(B)** Scaling refers to the process of adjusting the proportions or dimensions of an artwork when creating a replica or a larger or smaller version of the original. In the context of the replicated sculpture, scaling would involve accurately reproducing the size and proportions of the original artwork in the replicated version. This ensures that the overall composition and visual elements of the sculpture are maintained in the scaled replica. Exaggeration (A), casting (B), and balancing (C) are not specific techniques related to the replication process. Exaggeration refers to emphasizing or overstating certain elements in an artwork for artistic effect. Scaling refers to the adjustment of the proportions or dimensions of an artwork. Balancing refers to achieving a sense of visual equilibrium and harmony in an artwork's composition. Casting is a common method used in sculpture to create replicas or multiples of an original artwork. In the casting process, a mould is created from the original sculpture, and then a material such as bronze or resin is poured into the mould to create a faithful

reproduction of the artwork. This allows for the production of multiple copies of the original sculpture while maintaining its form and details.

13. **(B)** Edna Manley's "Negro Aroused" sculpture is known for its powerful portrayal of the struggles and resilience of Black people. It captures Manley's concern for the social and political issues faced by people of African descent, particularly in the context of racial inequality and discrimination. The sculpture represents a call to action and an expression of the artist's desire for racial justice and equality. While the other options may be relevant in certain interpretations or contexts, the depiction of the struggle for racial equality is the most commonly associated message with the "Negro Aroused" sculpture.

14. **(B)** Karabela is not the national dress of Antigua and Barbuda. The traditional dress of Antigua and Barbuda is known as the "Antiguan and Barbudan Wadadli Dress," which is a colourful and flowing dress typically worn during cultural events and festivals – It is a Madras dress. Options (A), (C) and (D) are correctly paired.

15. **(C)** Intuitive artists often work with found objects and materials, incorporating them into their artwork in unconventional ways. This approach aligns well with the use of recycled materials and objects, as it allows the artist to give new life and meaning to discarded items. The Caribbean region, with its rich cultural heritage and emphasis on sustainability, often inspires artists to create artwork that reflects environmental consciousness and resourcefulness. While other materials like marble and stone (A), metal and glass (B), and paints and canvases (D) are commonly used in art, the preference for recycled materials and objects can be seen as a distinctive characteristic of an intuitive artist in the Caribbean.

16. **(C)** Realism emerged in the mid-19th Century as a response to the rapid industrialization and societal changes brought about by the Industrial Revolution. Artists of the Realist movement sought to depict the world as it was, focusing on everyday life, social issues, and the realities of the working class. They aimed to capture the effects of industrialization on society, portraying subjects with a high level of detail and accuracy.

17. **(C)** Hector Hyppolite was known for his surrealist paintings. He was a Haitian artist who gained recognition for his unique style of painting that blended elements of Haitian Vodou (Voodoo) religion, folklore, and mythology with fantastical and dreamlike imagery. His paintings often depicted scenes from Haitian folklore, mythical creatures, spirits, and rituals. Hyppolite's works were characterized by vibrant colours, intricate details, and a surrealistic approach to composition. Surrealism is an art movement that emerged in the early 20th Century, emphasizing the exploration of the unconscious mind and the liberation of creativity. Surrealist artists sought to depict irrational and dreamlike imagery, often defying traditional conventions of reality and representation. Hector Hyppolite's work aligns with the principles and aesthetics of Surrealism, making him known for his contributions to the movement.

18. (C) The Edna Manley College of the Visual and Performing Arts was established in 1995. Located in Kingston, Jamaica, it is a premier institution for arts education in the Caribbean. It was named in honour of Jamaican sculptor and painter Edna Manley, who played a significant role in the development of Jamaican art. The college offers programmes in various disciplines, including fine arts, dance, drama, music, and arts education. It provides opportunities for students to pursue their artistic talents and develop their skills in a creative and supportive environment. The college has made significant contributions to the arts scene in Jamaica and has produced many renowned artists, performers, and educators.

19. (B) In Caribbean enslaved communities, music played a crucial role as a form of communication and resistance. Enslaved Africans brought with them their musical traditions, rhythms, and instruments, which became integral to their cultural expression and identity. Music served as a means of communication, allowing enslaved individuals to express emotions, share messages, and preserve their cultural heritage. Through music, they could communicate coded messages, coordinate activities such as escape attempts, and express their longing for freedom. Music also provided a sense of unity and community among enslaved individuals, helping them maintain their cultural traditions and spiritual practices. It served as a source of strength, resilience, and resistance against the dehumanizing conditions of slavery. Music became a powerful tool for preserving their cultural identity, instilling hope, and fostering a sense of belonging within the enslaved community. While music did provide entertainment and served as a form of expression, its significance went far beyond mere amusement. It served as a vital means of communication, cultural preservation, and resistance in the context of Caribbean enslaved communities.

20. (C) Oil painting is not considered a contemporary technological technique used in art. It is a traditional medium that has been used for centuries, particularly during the Renaissance and other historical periods. Oil painting involves the use of pigments mixed with drying oils, typically linseed oil, to create artwork. While oil painting continues to be practised by many artists today, it is not classified as a contemporary technological technique. On the other hand, augmented reality, virtual reality, and digital printing are examples of contemporary technological techniques used in art. These contemporary technological techniques have expanded the possibilities for artistic expression and engagement, offering new ways for artists to create and for audiences to experience and interact with artworks.

21. (A) The primary function of the pottery utensils created by indigenous Caribbean peoples was cooking and food storage. Pottery played a vital role in their daily lives, as it was used to make various types of vessels for cooking, serving, and storing food and liquids. These pottery utensils were often designed with specific features to meet the practical needs of food preparation and preservation. The clay vessels were shaped and fired to withstand heat, allowing for cooking over open fires or in earthen ovens. They were also effective in storing food, keeping it protected and preserved. The pottery utensils were essential tools for food preparation and played a significant role in sustaining the indigenous Caribbean communities. While pottery could also be decorated and have symbolic or cultural significance, its primary function was utilitarian rather than purely decorative or ceremonial.

22. **(B)** Canute Caliste's intuitive paintings primarily focus on the abstract interpretation of nature, particularly scenes from everyday life in Carriacou, Grenada. Intuitive art often emphasizes the artist's personal and spontaneous expression, and Caliste's works capture the essence of nature through abstract forms, colours, and compositions. His paintings may depict landscapes, flora, fauna, and other elements of the natural world in a non-representational or abstract manner, conveying a sense of the energy, vibrancy, and interconnectedness of the natural environment. While Caliste's work may incorporate elements of cultural, historical, or personal significance, the primary theme that stands out is his abstract interpretation of nature.

23. **(A)** The Jewish cemetery in Barbados is primarily associated with the Sephardic Jewish community. Sephardic Jews are descendants of Jews who originated from the Iberian Peninsula (Spain and Portugal) and were later expelled during the Spanish and Portuguese Inquisitions in the late 15th and 16th centuries. Many Sephardic Jews found refuge in various parts of the world, including the Caribbean. In Barbados, Sephardic Jews played a significant role in the island's early history, particularly in the sugar industry. The Jewish cemetery in Barbados contains the graves of Sephardic Jews and serves as a historical reminder of their presence and contributions to the island.

24. **(B)** The sculpture in the image is that of the Hanuman Statue located in the village of Carapichaima in Trinidad. The statue is situated on top of the Dattatreya Yoga Center and Mandir. Trinidad has a significant Hindu population and is known for its vibrant Hindu religious practices and temples. Options (A), (C) and (D) are not known for having a large Hindu population.

25. **(A)** The sculpture is associated with a mandir. A mandir is a Hindu temple or place of worship. It is a sacred space where Hindu devotees gather to worship deities and engage in religious rituals and ceremonies. The sculpture depicted in the image is likely found within a mandir, reflecting the religious and cultural traditions of the Hindu community in the Caribbean.

26. **(B)** The sculpture is associated with the arrival of East Indians through indentureship in the Caribbean. Indentured labourers from India were brought to the Caribbean as part of the indentureship system to work on plantations after the abolition of slavery. Their arrival had a significant impact on the cultural, social, and religious landscape of the Caribbean, and Hinduism became one of the prominent religions practised by the Indo-Caribbean community. The sculpture holds cultural and religious significance related to the history of the Indian diaspora and their contributions to the Caribbean region.

27. **(A)** The Dattatreya Yoga Center and Mandir upon which the statue is situated is built in a Dravidian style of architecture popular in South India. The Dravidian architectural style is primarily associated with the southern regions of India, particularly in the states of Tamil Nadu, Karnataka, Kerala, and Andhra Pradesh. It is characterized by its distinctively pyramid-shaped temple towers called gopurams, which are adorned with intricate carvings and sculptures of gods, goddesses, and mythical creatures. The temples in the Dravidian style often have large, enclosed courtyards and feature ornate

entrance gates. The use of vibrant colours and detailed sculptures is a notable feature of Dravidian architecture.

28. **(B)** In Hindu culture, the colour red is often associated with strength and bravery. It symbolizes courage, determination, and the warrior spirit. Red is considered a powerful and assertive colour that represents the ability to face challenges and overcome obstacles. It is commonly used in religious rituals and ceremonies honouring deities and heroes who embody qualities of strength and valour. The colour red is also associated with the Hindu god Hanuman, known for his incredible strength and unwavering devotion. In this context, red represents fearlessness and the willingness to face adversity with courage.

29. **(A)** The presence of a midden is typically a sign of human occupation. A midden refers to a deposit or accumulation of refuse or discarded materials, such as shells, bones, tools, and other artefacts, that accumulate over time as a result of human activities. These middens are often found in archaeological sites and provide valuable insights into past human civilizations, their diet, lifestyles, and cultural practices. Middens can be found near ancient settlements, campsites, or areas where people lived and engaged in activities like hunting, fishing, cooking, and toolmaking. By studying the contents of a midden, archaeologists can gain knowledge about the history and behaviour of past human populations.

30. **(D)** Intuitive art refers to artwork that is created without conscious planning or premeditation. It is characterized by a spontaneous and unstructured approach, often driven by the artist's instincts, emotions, and inner visions. Intuitive artists typically work in a free-flowing manner, allowing their creativity to guide them without strict adherence to traditional techniques or formal rules. The process of creating intuitive art is often described as a form of self-expression and exploration, where the artist taps into their subconscious mind and allows their instincts to guide the artistic decisions. The resulting artwork may be abstract, symbolic, or deeply personal, reflecting the artist's inner world and unique perspective.

31. **(C)** Cotton is the material most commonly associated with batik art in the Caribbean. Batik is a traditional textile art form that involves applying wax to fabric and then dyeing the fabric to create intricate and colourful designs. Cotton fabric is often preferred for batik due to its absorbency, which allows the dyes to penetrate the fabric evenly and create vibrant colours. Cotton also provides a smooth and durable surface for the application of wax and the subsequent dyeing process. While batik can be done on other types of fabrics such as silk or polyester, cotton is widely used and considered the traditional choice for batik art in the Caribbean and other regions.

32. **(A)** The most likely technique used to make crochets in the Caribbean is looping. Crochet is a craft technique that involves using a crochet hook to create interlocking loops of yarn or thread to form various patterns and designs. In the Caribbean, looping is the commonly used method for creating crocheted items. Looping involves pulling loops of yarn through other loops to create a fabric-like structure. It is a versatile technique that allows for the creation of intricate and detailed designs. Crochet has a

long history in the Caribbean and is often used to make clothing, accessories, and decorative items.

33. **(A)** The process of weaving where the weft thread is wrapped around the warp thread and then woven back is called tapestry weaving. In tapestry weaving, the weft thread is interlaced with the warp threads in a discontinuous manner, creating a weft-faced textile with the design or pattern formed by the coloured weft threads. The weft threads are wrapped around the warp threads to create the desired image or design, resulting in a dense and tightly woven fabric. Tapestry weaving is often used to create intricate and detailed pictorial designs, and it has been practised for centuries as a form of textile art. The other options are incorrect.

34. **(D)** Body painting is not typically used for medical treatments. While some cultures may use natural pigments or substances for medicinal purposes, it is not a common practice to directly apply body paint for medical treatments. However, body painting has been used for various purposes in different cultures throughout history. Body painting is often used in spiritual and religious ceremonies (A) to symbolize purification, connection with the divine, or as a form of prayer or ritual. It can be seen in practices such as tribal rituals, initiation ceremonies, and shamanic traditions. Additionally, body painting has been used by indigenous cultures as a form of camouflage during hunting or warfare (B). By painting their bodies with natural pigments and designs that blend with the environment, hunters could better conceal themselves from prey or enemies. Lastly, body painting is commonly employed in various celebrations, festivals, and cultural events (C). It serves as a means of expression, identity, and cultural pride. Festivals such as Carnival, Holi, and Indigenous cultural gatherings often involve body painting as a vibrant and festive adornment.

35. **(B)** Ceramics was a commonly used medium in the Maya culture for creating various objects, including pottery vessels and bowls. Maya artisans were skilled in pottery-making techniques, and they created intricate and detailed ceramic vessels for different purposes. These vessels were typically made by shaping and firing clay, resulting in durable and functional ceramic objects. The inclusion of a serpent design on the exterior of the bowl suggests the artistic and symbolic significance attributed to serpents in Maya culture, which often appeared in their art and mythology.

36. **(B)** The methods that might have been employed by the Mayans to create the serpent on the surface of the bowl are craving (II) and incising (IV). Carving involves shaping or cutting the surface of the material, in this case, ceramic, to create the desired design. Mayan artisans could have used carving techniques to carefully sculpt and shape the serpent image on the exterior of the bowl. Incising refers to the process of making shallow cuts or lines on the surface of the material. Mayan artisans might have incised the serpent design onto the ceramic surface using sharp tools or implements. This technique allows for more intricate details and precise lines. While firing (III) is an essential step in the ceramic-making process, it does not directly pertain to the creation of the serpent design on the bowl's surface. Sgraffito (I), which involves scratching through one layer of material to reveal another layer beneath, originated in Italy and is unlikely a method used by Ancient Indigenous societies.

37. (D) Impressionism, as an art movement, emerged in the 19th Century and is characterized by capturing the fleeting impressions of light and colour in a scene. While impressionist paintings do exhibit small, visible brushstrokes (A) and unblended colours (B) to create a sense of vibrancy and spontaneity, and they also aim to depict the effects of light accurately (C), they typically do not feature fragmented and abstracted shapes (D).

38. (B) Batik art is a traditional technique that involves applying wax to fabric and then dyeing the fabric. The wax acts as a resistor, preventing the dye from penetrating certain areas of the fabric. This process is repeated multiple times, with wax being applied and dyed in stages to create intricate designs and patterns. After the final dyeing, the wax is removed, revealing the colourful and patterned fabric. In batik art, artists use dyes specifically formulated for fabric, along with various tools to apply the wax, such as a tjanting tool or a brush. The fabric used for batik can be cotton, silk, or other natural fibres that can absorb the dye effectively. Therefore, Elizabeth, as a skilled batik artist, would likely be working with dye and fabric (B) rather than paint and canvas (A), knitting needles and yarn (C), or glue and paper (D).

39. (D) Appreciation, although an important aspect of engaging with art, is not considered a distinct step in the art criticism process. It is more of an ongoing attitude or approach that involves recognizing and valuing the aesthetic qualities, emotional resonance, and cultural significance of the artwork. The art criticism process typically involves several steps, including description, analysis, interpretation and evaluation. Description (A) involves objectively describing the artwork, including its physical characteristics, subject matter, and formal elements such as colour, composition, and technique. Analysis (B) occurs when the artwork is analysed and interpreted to understand its meaning, symbolism, and intended message. It may involve exploring the artist's techniques, cultural context, historical background, and artistic influences. Interpretation goes beyond analysis and involves making subjective connections and inferences about the artwork. It may involve exploring personal responses, emotional impact, and possible meanings behind the artwork. Evaluation (D) involves critically evaluating the artwork based on various criteria such as artistic skill, originality, creativity, conceptual depth, and overall effectiveness. It involves making judgments and forming opinions about the artwork.

40. (A) Formalism and contextualism are two different approaches to art criticism that prioritize different aspects of the artwork. Formalism, also known as formal analysis, emphasizes the intrinsic formal qualities of the artwork itself. It focuses on elements such as colour, line, shape, composition, texture, and other visual elements. Formalist critics believe that the artwork's aesthetic qualities and visual language are its primary sources of meaning and value. They often disregard or downplay external factors such as the artist's biography, historical context, or social commentary. On the other hand, contextualism in art criticism considers the artwork in relation to its historical, cultural, and social context. Contextualist critics believe that understanding the historical, cultural, and social circumstances in which the artwork was created is crucial to fully grasp its meaning and significance. They examine factors such as the artist's background, cultural influences, artistic movements, societal issues, and intended messages. Contextualism seeks to interpret the artwork by considering its broader cultural and historical implications.

CAPE®

ART AND DESIGN

MOCK EXAMINATION

Paper 01
1 hour 30 minutes

READ THE FOLLOWING INSTRUCTIONS CAREFULLY.

1. This Mock Examination consists of 40 items.

2. You will have 1 hour 30 minutes to answer them.

3. Each item in this Mock Examination has four suggested answers lettered (A), (B), (C) and (D). Read each item and decide on the best choice. Look at the sample item below.

Sample Item:

What is the process of creating designs on the surface of a ceramic vessel called?

(A) Glazing
(B) Incising
(C) Coiling
(D) Firing

Sample Answer:

The best answer to this item is "incising" and so (B) is shaded.

4. When you are told to begin, turn the page and work as quickly and as carefully as you can. If you cannot answer an item, go on to the next one and return to this item later.

RLF Publications.
"... redefining publishing..."

1. What was the name of the opening ceremony for the 1992 Barcelona Olympics that the Trinidadian Peter Minshall designed?

(A) "Rhythm of the Games"
(B) "Theatre of the World"
(C) "Carnival of Nations"
(D) "Festival of Fire"

2. Which of the following is NOT covered by copyright protection?

(A) Sculptures
(B) Paintings
(C) Ideas
(D) Photographs

3. Which of the following is an example of an icon in Caribbean art?

(A) A painting of a landscape
(B) A sculpture of a person
(C) A religious symbol
(D) A photograph of a building

4. Which contemporary technological technique allows for the creation of physical objects from digital designs?

(A) 3D printing
(B) Augmented reality
(C) Algorithmic art
(D) Virtual reality

5. Which art movement was influenced by Japanese art?

(A) Pop Art
(B) Renaissance
(C) Baroque
(D) Rococo

6. What is the subject matter of many of Hector Hyppolite's paintings?

(A) Vodou
(B) Landscapes
(C) Still life
(D) Portraits

7. What does the lotus flower symbolize in Hindu art?

(A) Purity and enlightenment
(B) Wealth and success
(C) Creativity and innovation
(D) Power and strength

8. Which was the likely technique used by Taino women to create baskets?

(A) Knitting
(B) Crocheting
(C) Twining
(D) Embroidery

9. A significant aspect of Caribbean intuitive art is that artwork is generally

(A) deeply personal and emotional
(B) technical depictions of human life
(C) based on political and social realities
(D) critically acclaimed and celebrated

Items 10 to 12 refer to the image below that reflects a colossal stone head that dates to 900 BC discovered in Central America.

Image is in the public domain and used pursuant to the Creative Common license. Source: https://commons.wikimedia.org/wiki/File:San_Lorenzo_Monument_4_crop.jpg (retrieved 30th November 2023)

10. The stone heads have generally been used to substantiate claims of African presence in the Americas in the pre-Columbian era because

(A) they depict strong negroid features
(B) Indigenous people did not have the tools to create stone heads on their own
(C) similar stone heads are found in Africa
(D) they do not resemble Indigenous people in Central America

11. Which of the following indigenous groups in Central America was associated with the stone heads?

(A) Maya
(B) Olmec
(C) Inca
(D) Aztecs

12. What material were the stone heads likely made from?

(A) Limestone
(B) Basalt
(C) Marble
(D) Sandstone

13. Which famous landmark in the Caribbean is a prime example of Gothic and Georgian architecture?

(A) Morne Fortune in Saint Lucia
(B) The Governor's Mansion in Jamaica
(C) The Red House in Trinidad and Tobago
(D) The Bridgetown Synagogue in Barbados

14. Which art period was heavily influenced by African art?

(A) Cubism
(B) Impressionism
(C) Baroque
(D) Rococo

15. Which Caribbean artist is famous for his lithographic works?

(A) Wifredo Lam
(B) Edouard Duval-Carrié
(C) Isaac Mendes Belisario
(D) John Dunkley

16. What is the significance of the traditional masquerade characters in Caribbean art and festivals?

(A) They are purely for entertainment purposes
(B) They represent cultural and historical traditions
(C) They are used to promote tourism
(D) They have no cultural significance

17. Which of the following UNESCO sites is located in Saint Lucia?

(A) Morne Trois Pitons National Park
(B) Brimstone Hill Fortress National Park
(C) Blue and John Crow Mountains National Park
(D) Pitons Management Area

Items 18 to 22 refer to the artefact below that was discovered in the Dominica Republic and dated c 1000.

Image is in the public domain.
Source: https://www.metmuseum.org/art/collection/search/312602
(retrieved 30th November 2024)

18. The artefact depicted in the diagram is referred to as a

(A) zemi
(B) duho
(C) batey
(D) macana

19. The likely medium for the artefact is

(A) wood and shell
(B) stone and marble
(C) glass and ceramic
(D) clay and sand

20. A defining feature of an artefact is that

(A) it is found in middens
(B) it is non-portable
(C) it is made by human beings
(D) it is made from animal remains

21. The Indigenous people who utilized the item in the diagram were the

(A) Aztecs
(B) Maya
(C) Taino
(D) Kalinago

22. Why is the artefact used in religious ceremonies?

I. To enter the spiritual realm
II. To represent gods and spirits
III. To ward off evil spirits
IV. To communicate to the gods

(A) I and II
(B) II and IV
(C) II, III and IV
(D) I, II, III and IV

23. Large-scale Hindu festivals are likely celebrated in all of the following Caribbean territories EXCEPT

(A) Grenada
(B) Guyana
(C) Trinidad and Tobago
(D) Suriname

24. Romanesque architecture flourished between the

(A) 5th and 10th Centuries
(B) 11th and 13th Centuries
(C) 14th and 16th Centuries
(D) 17th and 18th Centuries

25. Which of the following is a defining feature of Romanesque architecture?

(A) Rounded arches
(B) Ribbed vaults
(C) Wide windows
(D) Flying buttresses

Items 26 and 27 refer to the image below which reflects an archway designed in a particular architectural style.

Image is in the public domain.
Source: https:// //commons.wikimedia.org/wiki/File:Fig_46_bis_-Clerestory_opening,_nave_of_Paris,_showing_alterations.png (retrieved 30th November 2024)

26. Which architectural style is reflected in the design?

(A) Romanesque
(B) Gothic
(C) Baroque
(D) Victorian

27. Which of the following European countries originates the reflected architectural style?

(A) Germany
(B) Spain
(C) Italy
(D) France

---

28. Which of the following English-speaking Caribbean countries is known for its restrained version of a parish church built in the architectural style in the image?

(A) Jamaica
(B) Barbados
(C) Cuba
(D) Trinidad

29. Which of the following cenotaphs is located in Port of Spain, Trinidad and Tobago?

(A) The National Heroes Square
(B) The Memorial Park
(C) The Woodford Square
(D) The Castries Memorial

30. Which of the following Caribbean festivals is celebrated in Trinidad and Tobago and is known for its elaborate costumes, steel pan music and street parades?

(A) Holi
(B) Crop Over
(C) Carnival
(D) Junkanoo

31. Junkanoo is a festival that is associated with all of the following Caribbean countries EXCEPT

(A) The Bahamas
(B) Jamaica
(C) Belize
(D) Barbados

32. Which of the following architectural elements is commonly found in Caribbean plantation houses?

(A) Courtyards
(B) Turrets
(C) Flying buttresses
(D) Gargoyles

33. Which of the following architectural styles was most commonly adapted for churches in the Caribbean?

(A) Renaissance and modernist
(B) Gothic and baroque
(C) Georgian and neoclassical
(D) Modernist and Victorian

34. Which of the following organizations is responsible for organizing the annual Caribbean Festival of Arts (CARIFESTA)?

(A) Caribbean Tourism Organization (CTO)
(B) Caribbean Cultural Institute (CCI)
(C) Council on Human and Social Development (COHSOD)
(D) Caribbean Association of National Arts Trusts and Foundations (CANTA)

35. Which of the following terms describes a self-taught artist?

(A) Surreal
(B) Abstract
(C) Intuitive
(D) Realism

36. Which artistic technique involves painting with hot wax on a wooden surface?

(A) Encaustic
(B) Oil painting
(C) Watercolour
(D) Acrylic painting

37. Which Cuban artist is known for depicting Santería and its deities in their art?

(A) Manuel Mendive
(B) Eduardo Roca Salazar (Choco)
(C) Flavio Garciandía
(D) Antonia Eiriz

Items 38 to 40 refer to the image below which is a painting by the Italian artist Agostino Brunias of a Dominican linen market which was likely painted between 1750 and 1770.

Image is in the public domain.
Source: https://en.wikipedia.org/wiki/Agostino_Brunias
(retrieved 30th November 2024)

38. Based on the image, what was the likely motive of Brunias' artistic depictions of the Caribbean during the 18th Century?

(A) To capture the nuanced aspects of West Indian culture and daily life
(B) To expose the brutal conditions of slavery and the injustices of colonial rule
(C) To document the resistance and rebellions of enslaved people in the Caribbean
(D) To promote the economic success of the sugar plantations in the Caribbean

39. Having regard to the resources available in the 18th Century, which of the following BEST captures the breadth of Brunias' artwork in the Caribbean?

(A) Murals and wall paintings
(B) Ink and lithograph paintings
(C) Watercolours and oil paintings
(D) Sketches and acrylic paintings

40. In what way does Brunias' choice of subject matter and composition reflect the colonial attitudes toward Caribbean society during the 18th Century?

(A) His works focus on the integration of African people into European colonial systems as equals
(B) His portrayal of Caribbean landscapes and people conveys the idea of a harmonious and nonviolent colonial society
(C) His emphasis on the exoticism of Caribbean culture helped promote an image of the region as a paradise for Europeans
(D) His depiction of enslaved people performing domestic and laborious tasks reinforces colonial ideals of racial hierarchy and control

END OF TEST

ANSWER KEY FOR MOCK EXAMINATION

Item No.	Answer Key
1.	B
2.	C
3.	C
4.	A
5.	A
6.	A
7.	A
8.	C
9.	A
10.	A
11.	B
12.	B
13.	D
14.	A
15.	C
16.	B
17.	D
18.	A
19.	A
20.	C

Item No.	Answer Key
21.	C
22.	D
23.	A
24.	B
25.	A
26.	B
27.	D
28.	B
29.	B
30.	C
31.	D
32.	A
33.	C
34.	C
35.	C
36.	A
37.	A
38.	A
39.	C
40.	B

EXPLANATIONS TO ANSWERS FOR MOCK EXAMINATION

1. **(B)** The name of the opening ceremony for the 1992 Barcelona Olympics that was designed by Peter Minshall, a Trinidadian artist and designer, was "Theatre of the World." Minshall's vision for the ceremony was to create a theatrical production that celebrated the diversity and unity of the world's nations through the language of carnival. The ceremony featured a vibrant and visually stunning parade of performers, costumes, and larger-than-life puppets, blending elements of traditional carnival with contemporary artistic expressions. The concept of "Theatre of the World" emphasized the idea that the Olympics, like a grand theatre production, brought together people from all corners of the globe to participate in a shared spectacle of athleticism, culture, and celebration. The ceremony aimed to capture the essence of this global gathering and showcase the rich cultural heritage and artistic traditions of different countries. Through his innovative designs and creative direction, Peter Minshall brought a unique Caribbean flair to the opening ceremony, infusing it with the vibrancy, rhythm, and theatricality of carnival. The event received widespread acclaim for its artistic excellence and its ability to capture the spirit of unity and celebration that defines the Olympic Games.

2. **(C)** Copyright protection generally covers original works of authorship, such as sculptures, paintings, photographs, literary works, music, and other creative expressions. These works are protected by copyright laws, which grant exclusive rights to the creators, such as the right to reproduce, distribute, display, and perform their work. However, copyright does not protect ideas or concepts in and of themselves. Ideas, theories, concepts, or general knowledge cannot be copyrighted. Copyright protection extends to the expression of those ideas in a tangible form, such as a written document, a recorded song, or a painted artwork. In other words, it is the specific expression or manifestation of an idea that is protected, rather than the idea itself.

3. **(C)** In art, an icon typically refers to a religious symbol or image that holds special significance within a particular religious tradition. Icons are often used in religious practices and rituals, and they are believed to embody spiritual or divine qualities. They can take various forms, including painted images, sculptures, or symbolic representations. While all the options listed can be considered art, a painting of a landscape or a photograph of a building may not necessarily be classified as icons unless they hold specific religious or symbolic meanings within a religious context. A sculpture of a person could be an artwork but may or may not be considered an icon, depending on its purpose and significance within a religious or cultural context.

4. **(A)** 3D printing, also known as additive manufacturing, is a contemporary technological technique that allows for the creation of physical objects from digital designs. It involves layer-by-layer deposition of material to build a three-dimensional object based on a digital model or design. This process enables the production of complex shapes and structures that would be challenging or impossible to create using traditional manufacturing methods. Augmented reality (B) and virtual reality (D) are

not directly related to the physical creation of objects but instead involve digital simulations and overlays in the virtual or augmented space. Algorithmic art (C) refers to the creation of art using algorithms, but it does not specifically involve the physical production of objects.

5. **(A)** Pop Art was an art movement that emerged in the 1950s and reached its peak in the 1960s, particularly in the United States and the United Kingdom. It drew inspiration from popular culture, consumerism, and mass media imagery. One of the significant influences on Pop Art was Japanese art, specifically the influence of Japanese printmaking, such as ukiyo-e prints. Artists like Andy Warhol and Roy Lichtenstein were known for incorporating elements of Japanese art, including its bold colours, graphic style, and use of repetition, into their works. The Renaissance (B), Baroque (C), and Rococo (D) art movements were not directly influenced by Japanese art. The Renaissance was characterized by a revival of classical Greek and Roman art and culture, while the Baroque and Rococo periods were marked by elaborate and ornate styles that originated in Europe.

6. **(A)** Hector Hyppolite, a Haitian artist, was known for his vibrant and mystical paintings that depicted scenes inspired by Haitian Vodou, a syncretic religion that combines elements of West African beliefs and Catholicism. Hyppolite's works often featured spiritual and mythological figures, symbols, and rituals associated with Vodou. His paintings captured the essence of Haitian culture, folklore, and spiritual practices, becoming an important part of the Haitian art movement and contributing to the recognition of Haitian art on the international stage.

7. **(A)** In Hindu art, the lotus flower holds great significance and is often used as a symbol to represent purity and enlightenment. The lotus is associated with spiritual awakening, divine beauty, and the unfolding of one's higher self. It is often depicted as a blooming flower emerging from muddy waters, symbolizing the journey from ignorance to enlightenment. The lotus is also associated with various deities in Hinduism, such as Lord Vishnu and Goddess Lakshmi, further emphasizing its divine and auspicious nature.

8. **(C)** The likely technique used by Taino women to create baskets is twining. Twining is a weaving technique that involves the interlacing of weft strands over and under the warp strands in a specific pattern. Taino women would typically gather natural fibres such as palm leaves or grasses, prepare them by stripping and drying, and then use twine to create intricate and durable baskets. Twining allows for the creation of various designs, shapes, and sizes of baskets, depending on the specific needs and purposes of the Taino community.

9. **(A)** Caribbean intuitive art is often characterized by its deeply personal and emotional nature. Artists express their inner thoughts, feelings, and experiences through their artwork, creating pieces that are highly individualistic and reflective of their unique perspectives. The art is often created intuitively, without rigid adherence to formal techniques or traditional rules. It is a form of self-expression that allows artists to convey their emotions, experiences, and connections to their culture and environment.

10. **(A)** The stone heads discovered in Central America, particularly in the Olmec civilization, have been a subject of discussion and speculation regarding the presence of African influence in the Americas during the pre-Columbian era. One reason for this is that the stone heads depict features that are commonly associated with African or negroid physical characteristics, such as broad noses, full lips, and other facial features. These features have led some to propose that there may have been contact or migration between Africa and the Americas before Christopher Columbus' arrival. The interpretation of these stone heads and their significance is a topic of ongoing research and debate among scholars and archaeologists.

11. **(B)** The stone heads depicted in the image are associated with the Olmec civilization, an ancient Mesoamerican culture that flourished in what is now modern-day Mexico during the Preclassic period (approximately 1200–400 BCE). The Olmec civilization is considered one of the earliest complex societies in Mesoamerica and is known for its monumental architecture, including the creation of large stone heads. These stone heads, often referred to as "Olmec heads," are notable for their size and distinctive features, such as the elongated faces and stylized headdresses. They are considered iconic representations of Olmec art and cultural expression.

12. **(B)** The Olmec stone heads, including the ones depicted in the image, were primarily made from basalt. Basalt is a volcanic rock that is formed from the solidification of lava. It is a durable and dense material that was readily available in the regions where the Olmec civilization thrived. The Olmec artists would have carved these colossal stone heads using stone tools, shaping the basalt into the desired forms and features. Basalt was a preferred material for sculpting among the Olmec and is commonly associated with their artistic legacy. Limestone (A), marble (C) and sandstone (D) were not typically used by the Olmec civilization for their stone heads.

13. **(D)** The Bridgetown Synagogue, also known as Nidhe Israel Synagogue, is located in Barbados and is the oldest synagogue in the Americas. It is built in a unique architectural style that combines elements of Gothic and Moorish influences. The other options do not represent Georgian architecture in the Caribbean. The Morne Fortune in St. Lucia (A) is a historic hill and military fortification. The Governor's Mansion (B) in Jamaica, also known as King's House, is the official residence of the Governor-General of Jamaica. It is a grand mansion built in the neoclassical architectural style, featuring symmetrical design, columns, and a prominent entrance. The Red House (C) in the seat of Parliament in Trinidad and Tobago. It was built in the late 19th Century and features Victorian architectural elements such as ornate detailing, decorative trim, and a distinctive red colour.

14. **(A)** Cubism was a groundbreaking art movement that emerged in the early 20th Century and was heavily influenced by African art. Artists such as Pablo Picasso and Georges Braque drew inspiration from African tribal masks and sculptures, incorporating elements of African art into their own works. They were particularly drawn to the abstract and geometric qualities of African art, which challenged traditional Western notions of representation and perspective. The influence of African art on Cubism played a significant role in the development of modern art.

15. **(C)** Isaac Mendes Belisario, a Jamaican artist of Jewish Portuguese descent, is well-known for his lithographic works. He was active in the mid-19th Century and is considered one of the earliest known professional artists in Jamaica. Belisario's lithographs depicted scenes of everyday life in Jamaica, including landscapes, portraits, and cultural traditions. His lithographic prints were highly regarded for their detailed and accurate depictions, capturing the spirit and essence of the Jamaican people and their surroundings. Belisario's works have contributed to the documentation and preservation of Jamaican history and culture.

16. **(B)** Traditional masquerade characters in Caribbean art and festivals hold significant cultural and historical importance. These characters often represent various aspects of Caribbean folklore, mythology, and historical events. They embody cultural symbols, rituals, and traditions that have been passed down through generations, serving as a means to preserve and celebrate the rich heritage of the Caribbean. The masquerade characters can vary across different Caribbean countries and communities, but they typically carry deep cultural meanings and narratives. They may depict ancestral spirits, mythical creatures, historical figures, or representations of societal roles and customs. Through their vibrant costumes, masks, and performances, these characters bring to life the stories and traditions of the Caribbean people, serving as a visual and experiential expression of their cultural identity. Beyond their artistic and cultural significance, traditional masquerade characters also play a role in community celebrations and festivals, creating a sense of unity, pride, and connection among the participants and spectators. They contribute to the overall festive atmosphere and serve as a source of entertainment and education, allowing people to engage with and learn about their cultural heritage. While entertainment is certainly a part of the masquerade performances, their deeper significance lies in their representation of cultural and historical traditions, making them an integral part of Caribbean art and festivals.

17. **(D)** The Pitons Management Area in Saint Lucia is a UNESCO World Heritage site. It is located on the southwestern coast of the island and encompasses the iconic twin volcanic peaks known as the Pitons: Gros Piton and Petit Piton. These towering mountains rise dramatically from the Caribbean Sea and form a stunning natural landscape. The Pitons Management Area is recognized by UNESCO for its outstanding natural beauty, geological significance, and ecological diversity. It is home to a variety of unique plant and animal species, including rare and endemic flora and fauna. The area also includes pristine rainforests, coral reefs, and marine habitats. This UNESCO site in Saint Lucia attracts visitors from around the world who come to admire the majestic Pitons, hike the surrounding trails, and explore the natural wonders of the area. It is not only a symbol of Saint Lucia's natural heritage but also an important conservation area that aims to protect and preserve the ecological integrity of the region.

18. **(A)** The artefact depicted in the diagram is referred to as a zemi. A zemi is a type of religious object or deity in the Taino culture of the Caribbean. These objects, often carved from stone or wood, held spiritual significance and were considered sacred by the Taino people. Zemis were believed to embody spirits or deities and were used in religious ceremonies and rituals. They were seen as intermediaries between the human world and the spiritual realm, serving as a means of communication with the supernatural.

19. **(A)** The likely medium for the artefact depicted in the diagram is wood and shell. The Taino people commonly used natural materials such as wood and shells in their artistic and cultural expressions. Wood carving was a prominent art form among the Taino, and they created various objects, including zemis, from wood. The artefact may have been carved from a specific type of wood that was readily available in the region. The use of wood allowed the Taino artisans to carve intricate details and create unique designs. Additionally, the use of shells in Taino art is also significant. Shells were often incorporated into various decorative objects and served as symbols of spiritual significance. They were used for their aesthetic appeal and had cultural and symbolic value in Taino society.

20. **(C)** An artefact refers to any object that has been deliberately shaped or modified by human hands. It is created by humans for various purposes, such as tools, utensils, artwork, or ceremonial objects. Unlike natural objects that occur without human intervention, artefacts are intentionally crafted or altered by human beings. The act of creating an artefact involves the application of human knowledge, skills, and intentions. Whether it is a tool, a piece of artwork, or a cultural object, the human element is essential in its production. The deliberate shaping, design, and functionality of an artefact distinguish it from naturally occurring objects.

21. **(C)** The artefact depicted in the diagram, known as a zemi, is associated with the Taino culture. Zemis were sculptural representations of deities or ancestral spirits and played a significant role in Taino religious beliefs and practices. They were often made from materials such as stone, wood, or shell and were used in ceremonies, rituals, and spiritual contexts. The Taino people had a complex society and made significant contributions to the art, agriculture, and trade of the Caribbean region. However, their population declined rapidly after the arrival of European colonizers in the late 15th Century, primarily due to disease, forced labour, and violent conflicts. Today, efforts are being made to preserve and celebrate Taino cultural heritage and recognize its historical significance in the Caribbean.

22. **(D)** Religious ceremonies often involve the use of artefacts as significant objects of worship, representation, protection, and communication with the spiritual realm. Items I II, III, and IV are all reasons why the zemi was used in religious ceremonies in Taino societies. The zemi served as a sculptural representation of deities or ancestral spirits in Taino religious beliefs. It acted as a physical manifestation or symbol of these divine or supernatural entities, allowing worshippers to connect with and honour them during ceremonies. Additionally, the zemi may have been employed in Taino religious ceremonies to provide spiritual protection or to help dispel or repel evil spirits. The zemi was also used by Taino priests or spiritual leaders to convey messages, prayers, or offerings to the gods or to facilitate a connection between the human and spiritual realms.

23. **(A)** Hindu festivals are celebrated in several Caribbean territories due to the presence of significant Indo-Caribbean communities. Guyana, Trinidad and Tobago, and Suriname have substantial populations of Indo-Caribbean descent, and Hindu festivals are widely observed in these countries. However, while Grenada has cultural diversity and various religious practices, Hindu festivals are not as prevalent or widely celebrated compared to the other mentioned territories.

24. **(B)** Romanesque architecture emerged in Europe during the 11th Century and continued to flourish until the 13th Century. It was a prevalent architectural style characterized by thick walls, rounded arches, sturdy pillars, and small windows. This style was prevalent in the medieval period and served as a precursor to the Gothic architecture that followed. The term "Romanesque" itself reflects the influence of Roman architectural elements seen in the style.

25. **(A)** Rounded arches are one of the defining features of Romanesque architecture. They are characterized by semicircular or slightly pointed arches that span doorways, windows, and arcades. These arches are typically constructed using voussoirs, wedge-shaped stones or bricks, arranged in a radial pattern. The use of rounded arches was a departure from the earlier Roman architectural style, which predominantly featured the use of semicircular arches. Rounded arches in Romanesque architecture provide structural support and distribute weight more evenly, allowing for the construction of larger and taller buildings. Ribbed vaults (B) are a characteristic feature of Gothic architecture. While Romanesque buildings did incorporate windows, they were generally small and narrow in comparison to the large and expansive windows seen in Gothic architecture. Romanesque windows were often rounded or semicircular and featured simple tracery or no tracery at all. Flying buttresses are a distinguishing feature of Gothic architecture (D).

26. **(B)** Gothic architecture is characterized by several distinctive features, including pointed arches, ribbed vaults, flying buttresses, and elaborate ornamentation. These elements are often seen in the design of Gothic cathedrals, churches, and other religious structures. In the image provided, the pointed arches are visible, which is a key characteristic of Gothic architecture. Pointed arches allow for greater height and verticality in buildings, creating a sense of upward aspiration. The arches in the image are tall and slender, emphasizing the verticality of the design. While the image does not show other elements typically associated with Gothic architecture, such as ribbed vaults or flying buttresses, the presence of pointed arches is a strong indication of the Gothic style.

27. **(D)** Gothic architecture originated in France in the 12th Century and later spread throughout Europe. The development of Gothic architecture was influenced by the architectural innovations of French builders and the construction techniques they employed. Some of the most famous examples of Gothic architecture, such as Notre-Dame Cathedral in Paris and Chartres Cathedral, are located in France. These structures showcase the distinctive features of Gothic architecture and exemplify the mastery of French craftsmen during that period.

28. **(B)** Barbados is renowned for the John's Parish Church which was built using the Gothic architectural style in the 1640s. It was badly damaged by a hurricane and reconstructed in 1836. It showcases the classic Gothic style with its pointed arches, stained glass windows, and imposing structure.

29. **(B)** The Memorial Park is a prominent cenotaph located in downtown Port of Spain. It serves as a tribute to the fallen soldiers of Trinidad and Tobago who lost their lives during World Wars I and II. It serves as a gathering place for official ceremonies and remembrance events.

30. **(C)** Carnival is a vibrant and lively festival that takes place annually in Trinidad and Tobago, typically during February or March. It is characterized by colourful and extravagant costumes, energetic music, including the iconic steel pan, and large-scale street parades known as "masquerade bands." Carnival in Trinidad and Tobago is one of the most popular and well-known cultural events in the Caribbean, attracting both locals and visitors from around the world. Holi (A) is a Hindu festival celebrated in many parts of the Caribbean, including Trinidad, Guyana and Suriname. It is known as the "Festival of Colours" and involves throwing coloured powders and water at each other to celebrate the arrival of spring and the triumph of good over evil. Crop Over (B) is a traditional festival celebrated in Barbados which was originally celebrated to mark the end of the sugarcane harvest season. In modern times, it includes a series of events and activities, including calypso music, dancing, costume parades, and cultural exhibitions. Junkanoo (D) is a Bahamian and Jamaican festival celebrated on Boxing Day (December 26th) and New Year's Day. It features vibrant parades with participants dressed in colourful costumes, dancing to the rhythm of traditional music, including drums, cowbells, and whistles.

31. **(D)** Junkanoo is not traditionally associated with Barbados. It is primarily celebrated in the Bahamas, where it is considered the national festival. However, it is also celebrated in other parts of the Caribbean, such as Jamaica and Belize. It features vibrant parades with participants dressed in colourful costumes, dancing to the rhythm of traditional music, including drums, cowbells, and whistles.

32. **(A)** Courtyards are commonly found in Caribbean plantation houses. These open spaces within the house are typically surrounded by the main building or its wings and often feature gardens or outdoor areas. Courtyards provide a central gathering space and help with ventilation in the tropical climate of the Caribbean. Turrets (B), flying buttresses (C), and gargoyles (D) are architectural elements more commonly associated with Gothic or medieval architecture and are not typically found in Caribbean plantation houses. Turrets are small towers or projections that are often found on the corners or sides of buildings. They are commonly associated with castle-like structures. Flying buttresses are architectural supports commonly used in Gothic architecture to provide structural stability to tall walls. They are exterior arched supports that transfer the weight of the wall to a buttress or a support system. Gargoyles are decorative and sometimes grotesque stone figures that are often used as water spouts on the exteriors of buildings, particularly in Gothic architecture.

33. **(C)** In the context of the Caribbean, the most commonly adopted architectural style for churches is often a blend of influences, including Colonial, Georgian, and Neoclassical styles. These styles, characterized by symmetry, balance, and simplicity, were widely adopted for building churches due to their elegance and grandeur. While other styles like Gothic and Baroque might be found in some specific churches, Georgian and Neoclassical are the most common in the overall Caribbean context.

34. **(C)** The Council on Human and Social Development (COHSOD), a subsidiary organ of the Caribbean Community (CARICOM), is responsible for organizing the annual Caribbean Festival of Arts (CARIFESTA). CARIFESTA is a major cultural event that brings together artists, performers, and cultural enthusiasts from across the Caribbean region to showcase and celebrate Caribbean arts, culture, and heritage. COHSOD plays a key role in coordinating and overseeing CARIFESTA, ensuring its successful organization and execution.

35. **(C)** The term "intuitive" describes an artist who is self-taught or creates art based on their own instincts and personal vision, without formal training or adherence to traditional artistic conventions. Intuitive artists often rely on their innate creativity and intuition rather than following established artistic techniques or rules. They may develop their unique style and approach to art through experimentation and self-exploration. Intuitive art is characterized by its raw and authentic expression, often reflecting the artist's emotions, personal experiences, and inner world.

36. **(A)** Encaustic is an artistic technique that involves painting with hot wax. In this technique, pigments are mixed with molten beeswax and resin, creating a paint that is applied to a wooden surface. The wax mixture is heated to keep it in a liquid state while the artist works with it. Once applied, the wax can be manipulated using various tools and techniques such as brushes, knives, or heated metal tools. The wax solidifies quickly, allowing for layering and texture building. Encaustic painting creates a unique visual effect with a luminous quality and depth. The other techniques can be distinguished. While encaustic is specifically associated with painting with hot wax, the other techniques mentioned (oil painting, watercolour, and acrylic painting) can be applied using different materials, methods, and approaches. Oil painting (B) is a technique that involves mixing pigments with oil, typically linseed oil, to create a paint that is applied to a canvas or other surfaces. The slow drying time of oil paint allows for blending, layering, and creating smooth transitions of colour and texture. Watercolour (C) is a painting technique that uses transparent pigments suspended in water. The paint is applied to a surface, usually paper, with brushes and water, creating translucent layers of colour. Watercolour paintings often have a delicate and luminous appearance due to the transparency of the paint. Acrylic painting (D) is a technique that uses pigments mixed with acrylic polymer emulsion as a binder. Acrylic paint dries quickly and forms a permanent, water-resistant layer. It can be applied to a variety of surfaces, such as canvas, paper, or wood, and offers versatility in terms of texture and application techniques.

37. (A) Manuel Mendive is a prominent Afro-Cuban artist who incorporates elements of Santería, an Afro-Caribbean religion, in his artwork. His paintings, sculptures, and performances often explore themes of spirituality, nature, and cultural identity, drawing inspiration from the rich symbolism and rituals of Santería.

38. (A) Brunias' work often depicted daily life in the Caribbean, focusing on the interactions between enslaved people, indigenous groups, and European colonists. His paintings, like the linen market scene, aimed to capture the vibrancy of Caribbean society while often overlooking the harsher realities of slavery.

39. (C) Brunias was known for creating works in watercolours and oils, which were common mediums for artists in the 18th Century. His detailed depictions of Caribbean life, including market scenes, were often made using these techniques.

40. (B) Brunias' artwork often depicted a peaceful and orderly vision of Caribbean society, with enslaved people and indigenous groups shown in tranquil, non-confrontational settings. This approach reinforced colonial attitudes that sought to present the Caribbean as a harmonious and prosperous region under European control.

BIBLIOGRAPHY

Bailey, G. (2019). *Future Relics: Monumentalizing Afro-Caribbean Identity*. LAP LAMBERT Academic Publishing.

Barnet, S. (2015). *A Short Guide to Writing About Art* (11th ed.) Pearson Publishers.

Bethel, C. E. (1992). *Junkanoo: Festival of the Bahamas*. London: Macmillan Caribbean.

Boxer, D., & Poupeye, V. (1998). *Modern Jamaican Art*. Kingston: Ian Randle Publishers.

Cummings, A., Thompson, A., & Whittle, N. (1998). *Art in Barbados*. Kingston: Ian Randle Publishers.

Dempsey, A. (2011). *Styles, Schools and Movements: The Essential Encyclopaedic Guide to Modern Art* (2nd ed.). Thames & Hudson.

Douglas, R. (1996) *Caribbean Heritage – Architecture of the Islands*. Darkstream Publications.

Heywood, I., & Sandywell, B. (2017). *The Handbook of Visual Culture*. Bloomsbury Academic.

Janson, H. W., & Janson, A. F. (1997). *History of Art for Young People*. New York: Harry N. Abrams Incorporated.

Kirkham, P. (2013). *History of Design: Decorative Arts & Material Culture, 1400–2000*. Bard Center.

Nicholls, R. W. (2015). *The Jumbies' Playing Fround: Old World Influences on Afro-Creole Masquerades in the Eastern Caribbean* (Folklore Studies in a Multicultural World Series). University Press of Mississippi.

Northey, M., & McKibben, J. (2015). *Making Sense: A Student's Guide to Research and Writing*. Oxford University Press.

Poupeye, V. (2022). *Caribbean Art* (World of Art Series). Thames & Hudson.

Riggio, M. C. (2004). *Carnival: Culture in Action – The Trinidad Experience* (Worlds of Performance). Routledge.

Scott, N. (2009). *Compendium of Caribbean Artists and Art Forms*. In Press.

Strunk, W., & White, E. B. (1999). *The Elements of Style* (4th ed.). Pearson Plc.

Sued-Badillo, J. (Ed.). (2003). *General History of the Caribbean, Vol. 1: Autochthonous Societies*. UNESCO Publication.

Walmsley, A., Greaves, S., & Cozier, C. (2010). *Art in the Caribbean: An Introduction*. (In press). London: New Beacon Books.

Wilson, S. (1997). *The Indigenous People of the Caribbean*. Gainsville: University Press of Florida.

www.ingramcontent.com/pod-product-compliance
Lightning Source LLC
LaVergne TN
LVHW010354160826
845677LV00005BA/1270

* 9 7 8 9 7 6 9 7 1 7 9 8 5 *